A Journey to Becoming the Best-Self

Yvette Bodden

Black Rose Writing | Texas

2019 by Yvette Bodden
All rights reserved. No part of this book may be reproduced, stored in a retrieval system or transmitted in any form or by any means without the prior written permission of the publishers, except by a reviewer who may quote brief passages in a review to be printed in a newspaper, magazine or journal.

The author grants the final approval for this literary material.

First printing

The author has tried to recreate events, locales and conversations from his/her memories. In order to maintain anonymity in some instances, the author may have changed the names of individuals and places. The author may have changed some identifying characteristics and details such as physical properties, occupations and places of residence.

ISBN: 978-1-68433-319-6
PUBLISHED BY BLACK ROSE WRITING
www.blackrosewriting.com

Printed in the United States of America
Suggested Retail Price (SRP) $16.95

A Journey to Becoming the Best-Self is printed in Calluna

This book is dedicated to my daughter, Avani. You have been the light of my life since the day you were born. Bringing more laughter, joy and love to my heart than I ever thought possible. I feel enormous pride when I look at the young lady you are becoming. I am excited to see everything you do in the future. My biggest hope is that this book will demonstrate to you how we can turn a wish into reality by putting in the work. Life is a blessing, live it as such, every single day with Gratitude.

Acknowledgments

The initial idea of a book seemed surreal. For years, the endless pages floated in my head. But had not made their way onto my computer screen. This story was born after the storm clouds passed from my life. Stability and renewal were now present leading me to forge ahead with a possibility. A chance for others to read my words and connect with my pain. It meant so much to show others how it is doable. You can outgrow pain, become stronger wiser and more beautiful. Women are made to do this work. We just have to learn to withstand, push through and convert the pain. Create something worthy of the woman you are because the essence is already there to begin the labor of love. Self-love.

It is necessary to recognize the global *Awakened-Woman Community.* It would not have been possible to have written this type of book were it not for all the inspiration. I am sincerely grateful to hear your stories. Thank you for listening and allowing me to offer small pieces of wisdom that come from a personal place. My wish is to give you hope.

Writing a book has been one of the most rewarding challenges, thus far. It has taught me respect for the craft. It has also given life to a story. This is one of millions of stories written every day. Having the support of a village has been my rock. On or around my 40th birthday, I gathered a group of women together for a celebration of friendship and appreciation. I was joined by a small circle of empowered women. I nicknamed them my "garden of stones." Like family they held me up when my world was crashing down on me. The highlight created a trademark in my heart reminding me of strength. My squad had faith in me when I did not have it in myself. They embraced and cheered me on from the sidelines. They always knew I would come out on the other side of darkness.

I could not get through these pages without expressing gratitude for my two loves.

Avani, a rock throughout the writing gig, putting up with my sleep deprivation. My writing sprees happened at night leaving little time for sleep. It's difficult to be a morning person when the number of hours awake are higher than those of REM sleep. She pushed me to go hard, she dared me to never let go of the goal. Getting this book out into the world. You are my hero. My angel. The world love is not big enough to describe the emotion my heart holds for you.

Jeff, you came into my world when I did not believe in love. We spent many nights talking about how much I wanted to write this book. You told me, I could take this project on - you believed, encouraging me to remain true to myself. Work from the heart, own who I am as a woman. It helped me find confidence to do it all. I learned to love again but also to trust because of you. Thanks for being in my corner and being accepting without changing me. I love you babe.

My mom, sisters, brother and friends that have become family are my teachers. You have demonstrated fortitude and loyalty in ways not all experience. I'm thankful for having you on my side. Your guidance is one of dozens of blessings. Relationships go through phases but the last ones standing continue to flourish despite adversity.

There are those that come into your life to teach. I appreciate my father and ex-husband for making me confront some of love's most difficult lessons. A few of which drove me pen this book. Partly, I am stronger because of you. My mentors, Editor - Chelsey and Greg - Business Advisor. Your support during the writing of these chapters has been unbelievable. Generously offering time, skills and guidance to ensure I have the tools needed to succeed.

I take nothing for granted. The journey is ongoing. Don't think for a minute it stops. I continue learning like everyone reading this book. Hopefully, my story will empower, inspire and encourage others to own their story. Design a vision of the life you want to have then go for it!

A Journey to Becoming the Best-Self

Introduction

In May 2018, the world watched an American actress marry into royalty. The out-of-pocket cost of the fairytale wedding for her was probably $0. However, the price she's paying to have her happily-ever-after far exceeds any amount of money. She is giving up a normal lifestyle and identity to a certain degree. Now, we might not have to give up the freedom to say and do as we please but we hand over a part of ourselves in relationships. It may be fair to say that women give up a substantial amount of independence when they wed. We become wives, mothers and caretakers of the family clan. This leaves little to no time for personal development. There is an internal fight to retain the parts of us that have nothing to do with our husbands and children. Divorce unleashes a divine being after years of repression. Figuring out who you are and where you stand on your own should be a requirement to get married.

The amount of time spent with a spouse or significant other creates a microcosm of sorts. Your universe likely revolves around taking care of your home and everyone in it. Post-divorce, under the most normal of circumstances you are left with the responsibility of the kids during their daily routines. Despite the hectic schedules you still have a bulk of non-designated free hours to do as you please. Your friends are likely married with their own lives. If you have been a stay-at-home mom, you might feel the world moved at light speed which leaves you trying to catch up. Thoughts of restarting careers at a later stage in life is puzzling for anyone. Your schedule and all the active parts are up in the air. The world you're looking at has no gravity. So, what do you do now? Coming home with a list of things to do for your other half is no longer an obligation. A couple of days or even a week's break can be heaven-sent, until you find yourself somewhat lost. The role of wife has been deeply embedded in women's identity. Breaking out of the mold is work but worth the attempt. You will discover a new world about the woman you are. This exploratory period opens up a path to endless possibilities. We all have incredible strength, some unknown to us. One of the truest tests of inner power comes from pain. Embracing the process helps you in the long run. The old life left behind gives rise to a better you that won't need outside validation to be happy. This new woman will have the ability to build a foundation for a sturdy home while standing on her own two feet. Ultimately, whoever comes along to share your life should complement you instead of being your other half. You are complete and whole on your own.

The other dilemma we're left with when looking to regain our identity is that we have no clue where or how to begin the process. I read book after book hoping to find myself in one of them. The problem was that I couldn't identify with many of the people I was reading about. I wasn't independently wealthy nor did I come from an affluent family. My parents migrated from the Dominican Republic. My father made an earnest living from his job in a textile factory. He worked hard but spent the modest earnings with his friends once bills were paid. My mother helped to make ends meet by catering for family parties. The additional income from her gigs provided for the extras my brother and sisters received during childhood. Growing up, my mother taught me how to make something out of nothing. She used some of the added funds to pay for voice, guitar and ballet lessons. Starting at age 14, I held summer jobs to save my own money. Because of my mother, I understood of the importance of having money for a rainy day. Despite the knowledge, I did not plan for reality, as well as I should have, therefore, not having my ex-husband's income was a tremendous blow after divorce. I went from two incomes to a single in New York City with a child, nonetheless. A city named one of the most expensive in the country. Part of reclaiming my name meant acquiring a stronghold as provider for our daughter. I'd have to do this without extra financial help. I needed to figure out how to accomplish coming into my own holding down all roles successfully. Parts mother, career-professional and woman needed to be congruent in order to reach a state of genuine wellness. Trust, I had no idea where to begin the roadmap.

Humans are incredibly complicated beings. In a world of 7.6 billion people differentiated by geographical location, races, cultures, languages, religions, and customs we set ourselves up to find that one true love. We hope to find that one person that will love us with all our faults and bear witness to the rest of our lives. How tough is it to find that soulmate? The rigorous rituals and obstacles is enough for anyone to want to give up sometimes.

Divorce rates have remained relatively steady for years now. According to the APA (American Psychology Association) 40-50% of marriages end in divorce court. Will these numbers stop people from planning weddings with their mates? It most certainly will not discourage those wanting to get hitched! In 2017, the wedding industry had revenues surpassing $70 billion demonstrating there are plenty of couples still getting married.

Allow me to further deconstruct this for you to provide a better picture of the needle we're looking for in a haystack. Let's think about how different men and women are in every way. They are from Mars, we are from Venus, don't get it twisted, it's true! Our views vary widely on how we look at everything, particularly love. We come into a relationship with a different set of beliefs. Mold expectations of what we want, as well as, what we are willing to give. This is further complicated by experiences that can leave heavy baggage for a significant other to help carry. Then, there are those ideals we cherish. Place all these items in a crock pot and let them simmer, sprinkling in a pinch of personality. If we factor in these elements, would you agree finding the perfect mate to split our happy is a tall order? Getting it right on the first or second try is extraordinary. So, why be harsh on yourself if it does not work out? Divorce is painful but not fatal. It can be a transformational experience affecting men and women in very distinct ways. Men hurt but usually move away from the pain quicker. But both genders can make a choice to grow, learn and be stronger for it.

I have a tale of two divorces; the first one was a starter kit. There was a beautiful church, a groom and me (the bride) in an ivory, Sweetheart A-line wedding dress with princess seams. Yes, I can remember every detail of the bridal gown down to the bustle. I wanted to ensure I'd have no problems dancing the night away at my grand reception. Ask me about the groom and details get fuzzy. Many of us dream of our wedding day. We fantasize about the special moment with Prince Charming from a young age. It's no wonder the industry is raking up billions from our savings accounts. So much goes into organizing the details of such event. But how much time do we spend on selecting the best partner? If you pose the question to a sample of women, most are likely to provide us with a sensible answer.

There will also be pockets of women who might focus all their attention on the celebration itself instead of the groom. It's one of the reasons we have the Hallmark Channel! Guilty as charged, I genuinely cared about my groom, just not enough to spend the rest of my life with him. A sea of red flags waved across my lawn. I ignored every single one. The wedding became bigger than him, it should have signaled trouble ahead. I ignored the signs, dismissing anything that didn't align with my fairytale. I hand-picked all the specifics to make it the perfect wedding. The groom offered no say. He did not care to provide an opinion on invitations, guests, dress, tuxedo, venue, menus or wedding rings.

Honestly, I should have known then and there something was off but I kept the motor running. The race to the altar was on! It was no wonder the party ended less than a year later with divorce papers and a relocation for him. Did it hurt? Yes, but I wasn't exactly feeling like I had lost my place. The euphoria of my 20s and lack of experience led me to take a chance on something that was bound to break. The foundation wasn't there to hold the structure down in place. A divorce was finalized quickly, as there were no financial or emotional wounds to nurse. I didn't realize how fortunate I was to cut ties, getting a fresh start. I walked away unscathed waltzing into the next chapter of womanhood. This next crossroad took me on an extremely difficult journey testing my force and self-love.

All of us have an individual roadmap to follow. Our own set of lessons to accomplish during a lifetime. Each person manages the tutorial at their pace, generally forcing a repetitive pattern of mistakes until the mission is completed. The faces, names, and situations put in place can change but the moral of the story you're looking to achieve will remain until you find your truth.

A few years following my divorce, I married again. I was very much in love. The feelings for this man ran deep. He took over my soul navigating the inner trenches. Have you ever felt like one with someone? I did – grateful to have been able to give in to such a powerful emotion. The wedding was quite simple, an intimate affair. A group of four – the two witnesses and us. If marriages carried an indemnification clause, I would have struck it rich. Not having a costly celebration resembling a drive-thru pick-up of "I-Do's" was one of the smartest decisions made in love. I marked my 30th birthday with a notion that life was under control. This girl was ready to skip to a new chapter. I had my own place in Manhattan and a good job in the financial industry to support a modest lifestyle.

I let myself fall head over heels in love with a good man. Although, he was not the right man for "Me," there was an immense amount of love. It's all that mattered. When I say, "Me" keep in mind, I'm using the term loosely. I was floating through life without true purpose with no clue who "Me" was at the time. My sole happiness was making others happy, which did not leave room for my needs. Despite inner struggles, I was glowing and very much in love. A man with many virtues – not perfect, but who is? Honest and caring providing security in our home. He made me laugh and cherished parts of me giving me infinite moments of joy. I was able to show him glimpses of the real me but not entirely. There were compromises as in every relationship. I was willing to make sacrifices for the sake of love. We were inseparable during our courtship. Love's exhilaration carried us for years. Conflict does not exist when there are no opposing sides. I made it my second job to avoid the waves creating a home close to perfect – in my mind, anyway. There was plenty of love to go around. The gift of a daughter gave all the reason to completely excuse myself from having my own identity. Having the roles of wife and mother while holding a full-time job was everything. In my mind these things defined me. Over the course of close to a decade, juggling the responsibilities of being everything to everyone consumed me. It made me weary, draining the some of the glee out of my body. The tide began to turn creating a wave of internal turmoil. The woman began to disappear from the family picture. I'd become someone I didn't like or recognize. Questions began seeping into my mind that affected my reality. I wasn't sure if I was prepared for the answers but owed it to myself to begin the quest of self-discovery.

Being a woman is a beautiful gift. Though this wonderful honor bestowed upon us also carries immense responsibility. It's not to say that men don't have them but we tend to carry the weight of tradition. During the earlier years as families began to structure themselves, extended families were the norm. The idea of a nuclear family consisting of traditional roles of father, mother and children was not dominant. In fact, it was not until around the 1920s that the roles of male breadwinner and female homemaker began to flourish. Until that time, families were made up of groups creating a unit which shared the responsibilities of caring and providing for the home and children in it. Today, the roles are once again evolving. The variety of households presented in today's society run the entire spectrum. This can make things confusing as we continue cultural diffusion.

I'll make myself an example, as I'll do throughout this book. Hopefully, it will help you understand how I came to build this idea in my head of how things are supposed to be done. My parents married young and came to the United States from the Dominican Republic shortly after their nuptials. Being the oldest of four siblings, these memories could be slightly tainted but intact for the most part. My mother loved my father very much in spite of all his faults. They raised us in a relatively traditional home. She cooked, cleaned and took care of our home while he went off to work his 8-5 each day. He provided basic necessities for the household. She stayed home making sure everyone had what they needed. One of my most vivid memories I have from children include one of my father walking in from work to find his dinner ready to be served after his bath. Now, when I tell you dinner was served, I mean it! My mother would greet him and serve his dinner tray of food placed neatly in front of him. He seldom ate at the dinner table being he worked on his feet all day at the factory. I watched the same pattern for years until the day they called it quits. I grew up believing this was the proper way to take care of your partner by making sure all his needs are met. I was too young to process that my mother's needs were the ones not being taken care of.

How many of us women tend to everyone else surrendering our own desires? We do it without so much as a sign of appreciation, selflessly. Recognition on the yearly Mother's Day is a highlight. It is not easy to give so much but we take care of our loved ones out of devotion and responsibility. We love our roles even if at times they strip us of our identity. Some women learn to do so from a very young age by watching it happen at home. I was able to assume all the roles in my home for close to 10 years. My ex-husband took care of his end, contributing when it was possible. Changing diapers, helping start dinner. No matter how much he tried, it never seemed to be enough. I felt the burden of the roles crowding me. It left days short on breaks to take a breath in between chores. We all have a threshold that is safe until the levees burst. Mine left an overflow of emotions, maybe resentment. It was the turning point that warranted me asking for my share. I was ready and deserving of it. I needed to find me again for fulfillment.

One Sunday afternoon while my husband was out with our daughter. I found myself at home alone totally off track. The thoughts of life as it was drowned me. Looking around my living room, I saw nothing but pictures of a perfect family. A beautifully decorated dining table dressed with flowers. It complemented the brightness of the sunlight that came in through our windows. The love for my family became bigger than me. I had no idea who I was anymore. The things I wanted started to matter. The woman had been overshadowed by the responsibilities of being a mother, wife and caretaker. Living with fragments of myself was eating me up inside. It felt like my identity was being stripped away. I did not know how to stop this runaway train. The anxiety brought on by the feelings overwhelmed me. My heart was beating out of my chest. The shortness of breath brought on intense fear. The breakdown caused my body to tremble forcing me to snap. A call to my sister assisted me off the ledge that day. The incident that took place confronted me with a harsh reality. I had to figure myself out. It was dire to find out who I was on my own without them.

The troubles coming from that realization destroyed the relationship from the inside out as he wanted the girl he married all those years ago. The core was solid, same woman was still there with feelings intact. However, I wanted to reintroduce myself to society as an individual, an empowered woman. The desire to have my own life within the confinements of the institution produced bitterness. Being whole again, meant reconnecting with friends and having personal time. The request fell on deaf ears. The conflict between what he wanted and what I was able to give was skewed. Increasingly, the upheaval at home became too much to bear. The marriage could not resist the fracture. While I sensed the walls were closing in on me, I wrestled with what was happening. He was slipping away or I was letting go little by little.

My heart was breaking piece by piece as I watched a fantasy crumbling before my eyes. We got married with the ideal that death would do us part. The notion that the only thing to separate us from our greatest love is to put one of us 6 feet under is bit scary. But these words are inserted into millions of vows every year. Many days, we joked about buying matching rocking chairs to place them side by side on our porch and watch sunsets after our daughter went off to college. I had found my person in a world of billions. A witness to my life. The one to share the good and bad so I would not walk alone. My soul went dark on the realization that a promise to be together forever would never be. Our dream was dying. A divorce was looming. There was nothing else we could do to fix it. Failed attempts at communication, couples counseling and interventions could not save us. We passed a point of no return. Discontent steadily took over our home.

I wanted to make it work and there was fight left in me for my family. I just could not do it alone. We had to meet halfway, in the middle of each other's needs. People say marriage is 50/50. Truth is a partnership requires 100% effort from both sides. I was willing to put in the work making the necessary compromises. He was not interested to embrace my evolution. Resistance on both sides were a breeding ground for situations that put us in a tug of war. The struggle of power in the household begins early in a relationship. Have you tried to take the remote control from your spouse, boyfriend or partner during a football game? Yes, the struggle is real.

The euphoria experienced when love takes hold is similar to the strength of a thousand men. Ironically, we describe it as "falling in love." But the feeling is the complete opposite – it will lift you as you visualize a power higher than yourself. Most of us would do anything to make the other person happy including give up power. We surrender control of sound, mind, and body. It does not sound entirely sensible, does it? Some argue it's a chemical reaction while others state it is a heartfelt emotion which cannot be defined by the mind. Whatever way you define it, we cannot deny that it makes us act in crazy ways. In my case, I know it made me relinquish my power as a woman. My opinions, freedom of thoughts were curtailed to accommodate someone else's happiness. The relationship dictated the way I lived my life to a degree. My love for him was everything. The light within was dimmed to spotlight him. I was in love with love, with the ideal of what a family was supposed to look like. But at what cost? It was stealing my authenticity which I was no longer willing to hide after years together. We agreed to disagree – cut our losses, ended things. There was no middle ground for him while I refused to revert to the part of the submissive. Ironically, we were crazy for each other but it did not suffice which was more hurtful. Rather than drag out years of unhappiness, we decided a separation was best to minimize damage. Divorce papers were filed. It was not what we would have chosen but life seldom gives us what we want. It is likely to put us on a path of what we need, even if we don't know it at the time.

PART I: DIVORCE HAPPENS

A decision to separate is not made lightly. You will find that it affects every aspect of your life and all those in it. People spend years in discontentment to avoid the repercussions that follow a breakup. Once the words come out of your mouth delivering the news, waves of aftershock hit the pavement. The impact experienced will be unique for every family, in most cases, devastating. Assets accumulate as time accrues. Everyone is emotionally vested in the relationship. The children, if any. The parents, grandparents, mutual friends and family all wondering how they will survive the aftermath of loved ones' separation.

When news of divorce hit the press, my soon-to-be ex-husband's family kept their distance. In some way their actions made sense or I was rationalizing. The fact remained, they did not want to be part of the mess. They adopted me as kin for the duration of the relationship then dropped me like a hot potato after revelation the marriage was doomed. It is one of the side effects of divorce. Inevitably, family and friends take sides until the chaos passes. Our circle of friends consisting of his allies left me without rights to seek them for comfort. The line in the sand had been drawn. Loyalties would stay on pertinent sides of the fence. Luckily, I had my sisters and mom on my side. Our daughter was about four-years-old at the time and never felt the effects of the divorce. We made every effort to shelter her as much as possible. The goal was preserving her mental health no matter the cost. If we could maintain some sort of normalcy it would help damage control. We were already carrying the guilt of her world being turned upside down. How do you explain to your baby (or babies) that their parents are better separated than together? Firstly, you do so very carefully. Keep the story simple with minimal details. Too much information is a burden that no child should have on their shoulders. Adults make the decision to make a commitment to one another. When ties are severed, same rules apply. The children should not be added to the equation – ever. Uttering the word "divorce" alone gives us a bad feeling. It's associated with conflict, animosity, anger, sadness and plenty of negativity. My mother's parents ended their marriage, as did mine. Her brothers and sister also had broken vows. On my father's side, there were was unity and endurance. The women suffered more to keep their marriages and homes intact. There is no easy path, it is hard work. Obviously, a history of divorce in my family had an effect on me but did not entirely make me reject marriage. Although, my parents were not successful it did not take away from what marriage meant to me. It signifies a promise of love, respect, commitment and acceptance of my chosen partner. Unequivocally, it is not a vow to put up with mistreatment or abuse of any kind. My signature on the certificate does not grant permission of ownership. I wanted to be my own person in charge of my identity as a woman. My partner was not allowing me to be me. How could I then be with someone who was not willing to receive the person evolving when the pure essence of who I was never changed? Sacrificing my need to find out who I truly was as a person was not worth the cost of admission. It's when I knew divorce was eminent. Neither side was going to budge. Negotiations were over before they even began, sadly.

    The initial thought after my realization was "Now What?" I had been in love with the same man for a decade. We had a family, home that I loved and felt safe in – what would happen to us without him?

Who would protect us? A sea of emotion submersed my soul once reality set in – rational and irrational. The feelings ranged from great sadness to anger, mainly guilt. The pain of losing my husband was excruciating causing paralyzing trepidation. The thoughts that I would not be able to move on without him were haunting. My heartstrings tugged at me every day. It all seemed surreal. The best way to describe it would be to imagine a nightmare rollercoaster ride that you can't get off of.

You may be familiar with the Five Stages of Divorce Grief. The stairway to hell and back include Denial, Anger (Pain/Fear big part of it), Bargaining, Depression and Acceptance. I paid a visit to all stages during the grieving period. Some stages lasted longer than others. Loss is traumatic. Losing a loved one puts things into perspective and death has no remedy. However, divorce can produce similar feelings of grief. We feel deprived of love and not having the comfort of an old life. The next phase of the journey would be a walk through my own Dante's Inferno. Each stage dragged me down further, increasingly deepening the wounds and heartbreak.

This Can't Be Happening to Me!
(DENIAL)

We can give our all to save love, sometimes still ending up with nothing. Everyone has an internal voice. The one that tells you the moment has come to cut your losses. Reasons for the breakup vary from couple to couple. Whatever the reason, it is a difficult pill to swallow, especially when you do not see it coming. The denial stage usually begins while you're still in the relationship. We choose to ignore the signs or red flags. I consider myself lucky. Once the metamorphosis started for me, instinctively I knew that it would be a struggle. He inherited a dominant, old school mentality, hindering him from opening his eyes to the situation unfolding. I wanted us to grow together not apart. I felt I had done things the right way. It was impossible for me to believe it was ending this way. Maybe he wanted a way out? It seemed in my eyes he threw the game without a good fight. Maybe, pride was stronger than his love? It is what I like to hold on to because admitting he was not as vested in the relationship caused great pain. There are two sides to every story, this is the interpretation of mine.

    The refusal to admit to myself or others it was over delayed the healing process. One afternoon, the soon-to-be ex asked to pick up our daughter after school. We were not particularly friendly but thankfully the animosity did not force us into a ring of fire. He blamed me for the ordeal since I changed without warning. He believed my act of selfishness cost the marriage. The initial visit to the house since our separation was tough on all of us. I got our baby girl ready and took the elevator down to see her off for the weekend with her father. On our way down, one of the neighbors from another floor entered the elevator. She kindly greeted us "How are you? You make such a beautiful family. How many years have you been together?" In that moment, I felt as if someone punched me in the gut. I briefly looked at him, responding "Thank you, Mrs. Greenberg. We've been together 10 years." The trip downstairs took seconds but felt like minutes that lagged in silence after that statement. I did not have the courage to mention a separation or say anything out loud that would reference divorce because it would make it true. Our families knew of the issues we were having at home. They respected our space instead of meddling. I'm not sure if it was good or bad but the tension at home cut like a knife. What I did know for sure was that my heart had not caught up to my brain. It was hard for me to accept we were headed for divorce court. I began to pull away from family and friends alike out of shame. I reserved my feelings, keeping conversations to a minimum. Denial and avoidance became close allies. Not sure it made things easier. But it's how I learned to temporarily cope with the mess.

Emotional Agony that Cuts like a Knife
(ANGER fueled by Pain and Fear)

Eventually, it all becomes too real. Repressing or denying reality will take us, so far. The next stage was a mesh of emotional suffering. The psychological lacerations of pain, fear, and anger are almost impossible to separate when reeling inside the vortex of divorce. Humans are courageous souls. Women are trained early on to withstand several types of pain. At an early age each month, nature physically prepares us for womanhood. We are given the capability to give life. Our bodies go through a transformation of sorts resulting in birth. But enduring the torture of heartbreak can be a lot for the mind. It takes its toll on the bravest of soldiers. Until we make a conscious decision to fight.

    Causes for ending a marriage vary among couples. Some relationships deteriorate from wear and tear over time. You will find some that mutually agree to dissolve the union. However, a bulk of divorces are a result of relationships crushed by betrayal, identity loss, lack of intimacy or financial troubles. These breakups can leave a trail of disenchantment, unhappiness or relief. Ramifications differ from person to person due to a list of variables. Some put on a courageous face functioning normally with minimal effect to their emotional state. Others have their lives thrown into a tailspin of financial or emotional devastation. Either can be scarring, resulting in serious consequences. Countless cases over the years have shown men and women demonstrate severe degrees of desperation after breakups. News reports provide us with enough examples of individuals distraught by separation and divorce.

June 2016 in Las Vegas, NV – After a woman filed for divorce, a man shot her and their three children before taking his own life.

June 2017 in Lancaster, PA - A woman killed herself and 2 young children during a bitter divorce. Ultimately, burning down their home leaving a family to deal with the tragedy.

July 2017 in Greenville, SC – A woman murdered both her small children, as well as, her estranged husband's girlfriend. The couple had been in the process of a contentious divorce fighting for custody.

January 2018 in Crawfordsville, IN - A woman fatally stabbed both of her little ones and herself after husband filed for divorce. She survived the self-inflicted attack.

February 2018 in Tampa, FL – Days before she filed for divorce and freezing assets to stop him from leaving her destitute, a man shot his wife of 22 years following an argument.

Of course, these are acute incidents of emotional pain experienced by both genders. A variety of factors play into situations such as mental health issues and relationship history to name a few. Do people have the potential to conduct themselves very badly? Psychologists say it is possible to snap under certain circumstances. There are people with severe attachment problems or fear of abandonment tracing back to childhood. Crippling panic can push someone already in a precarious state to dangerous rage. The pain is real and should not be ignored. If you feel vulnerable to someone who makes you afraid, best thing to do is seek help from a trusted family member, friend or authorities. It is just as crucial to recognize when you do not feel right. If you think you can be harmful to yourself or loved ones, it is imperative to find someone – anyone – who can help talk you off the ledge.

A breakup can cause significant hurt but we are capable of overcoming. Pain, dread, and hostility are all part of the dissolution process. We need to let ourselves feel these things to move on to the next part of healing. I did not have a true understanding of the concept until things took a turn. Almost a year passed before acknowledging the inevitable. I morphed into a human. Years of marriage immersed me in the role of a "Yes Monster." My acceptance of what others wanted, no matter the cost had become my truth. What I wanted or needed did not appeal to me as much as my family's happiness. Time arrived to release resentment of whatever had been holding me back. I was angry the marriage had an unfavorable outcome. Upset at myself for being in the situation I was in – alone. I was terrified of the next steps required to secure the financial health of my young daughter and myself. I was incredibly sad that the man I loved so much let me down. Destroyed by the extinguishing of a dream. The family unit we created vanished. Castles in the sky imploding leaving me in shambles. There was a lot of pressure to perform for the people around me and keep it together to ensure our little girl felt safe. The spiritual rollercoaster was a ride of highs and lows that could make or break me. But I am still here.

You are entitled to mourn the end of a relationship. Cutting ties with an old life has an intense level of difficulty whether it's been one year or decades together. Everyone heals at a different pace. Setting a timeline for your pain is unrealistic. You have to decide the degree of comfort required for your peace of mind. I was never at ease feeling angry. It was an emotion to avoid because of the household I was raised in, a home full of volatility. My parents fought tons about everything. Their combative relationship fueled my fear of confrontation as an adult. It also made me reject any feelings that could contribute to a combative environment. I dealt with it by wearing a poker face, holding back emotions. Refusal to express my displeasure had a negative effect on me, personally. While riding the coaster of frustration and outrage for a couple of years after separation. I managed to retreat to a familiar place that saved me during childhood. I relied on the ability to numb myself of painful feelings. The numbness is blissful ignorance to a point. It did not pan out well for me.

Disconnecting emotionally, also led to pushing down any joy I could feel. Removing myself from feeling anything made me cold but protected me. It's how I rationalized the behavior. Does it sound confusing? Imagine the lightning bolts striking my psyche at this time. Shutting it down was the only way for me. My mind developed its own defense mechanism to help me get through the hurdle. Indifference got me through work and home, relatively unscathed with exceptions. The problem with this tactic is that we can't numb ourselves of one feeling without nixing others in the process. We do not get to pick and choose what we can or cannot feel. Human beings are made to feel. Emotional numbness was exhausting, it took a great deal of energy without understanding to what lengths it was damaging me. I was pissed off that my life was turning out this way and afraid of spending the rest of it alone. Unable to make it work and feeling like a failure were two of the hardest things to deal with during this stage. Forgiving myself wasn't in the cards for a long while. The next part of my voyage transported me to places internally necessary for self-discovery.

The difficulty of letting go of who I was in order to become this cold person was dreadful. The level of avoidance acquired scared me. I fought with all my might to learn the art of resistance. Pushing away anyone attempting to get close to me became second nature. Trust was hard to come by. No one could break down the wall built around my heart. I let my guard down at home where I was safe. My daughter grounded me daily. She made me feel human, allowing me to have moments of vulnerability. I found myself looking for outlets to release the negative energy. I knew that if I did not find ways to release the anguish inside, I would find myself in a lost world. The first thing to do was find a project. Something to focus on outside of work and daughter. The apartment we were living in was filled with memories. The marriage ended but a hefty trail of bills still needed to be paid. Rent, utility, car and credit card payments were to be taken care of, one way or another. Securing finances was the priority. Now, a sole wage-earner at home, pressure was insurmountable. The baggage left intensified my outrage. Despite life spiraling out of control like Dorothy's house in *The Wizard of Oz,* I could not afford to let myself be swept away by the tornado.

I repeatedly heard the words "God never gives us more than we can handle." It is a quote by Debbie Ford, American author who wrote motivational books. As much as I appreciated the cliche as a way of encouragement, my response to the statement, "Are you serious – Are you kidding me, right now?" I was visualizing myself in quicksand without a hand to get me out of the hole. Terrified of failing by not being able to provide the life my daughter deserved was emotionally crippling. An unknown future awaiting buried my head in worrisome thoughts. I was scared of the inability to manage the routine responsibilities on my own. Doubtful, I could carry a household on my shoulders without financial assistance. Nights alone in a bed bought for two was too much to bear. The fears were everywhere in and out of my sleep.

People will try to be supportive which is kind. Remain humble to those that stand beside you at this tough time. But, also remember that you are entitled to grieve your loss. Do not obligate yourself to feel better in the name of pleasing others. It is essential to maintain your mental and physical well-being to have the greatest chance of surviving any breakup.

Taking care of your suffering is necessary to regain balance in your life. This stage was perplexing because the exasperation pumped my body with adrenaline but drained me mentally. Undoubtedly, I knew the key to getting out of this hardship was getting my head back in gear. It all begins upstairs – if your mind isn't straight everything begins to fall into a dark abyss. Digging my head out of it was not easy but with effort and determination, I began to acquire equilibrium. Step by step starting to get out of my own way. Not to say the ugly feelings disappeared, right away. It helped to acknowledge the emotions being experienced, as it was part of the healing process. I was in my right to feel the anger, now I had to figure out how to use that energy productively.

One of the most difficult things to do is move out of your own way to allow good to take over. We all have "life stuff" thrown our way to shake us up. Challenges big and small overwhelm making us feel powerless. During this period control of matters slipped through my fingers. Having a child changes everything. I could not afford to let her down, she depended on me. Silencing the critical voice in my head would encourage the shift I was trying to achieve. Acknowledging obsessive thoughts was also part of the blueprint. The tasks were in no manner simple, they were taxing. The activity involved drowning out the internal voices that were working against me. Eliminating judgment and replacing it with kindness inward. The exercise was a long mental exercise. Talking myself out of dark places in my mind took an enormous amount of boldness and self-love. I cleared pathways leading to a better place. Agitation and desperation were not fully wiped out but became manageable making me a little bit stronger every day.

The next two years would be the loneliest and scariest after blowing up the marriage. While my daughter was away with her father on weekends, I was dealing with my crazy. Plans for our move from New York to Connecticut were being solidified. Now, a single working mother, I had to reduce expenses to survive. My job saved me, giving me something else to focus on outside of personal drama. A career as an assistant is not always the most lucrative but pays a decent salary. Losing a secondary income was a strike but I had a game plan. It could have been worse were it not for my mother's advice years ago. I took my first summer job at the age of 14 as a clerical assistant. On my first payday, mom sat me at the kitchen table. A mother of three girls looking to make sure she prepared us for the future there were many pep talks. I sat across from her, anxiously waiting for her to speak. We mainly spoke Spanish at home, but she would pull out the English occasionally. "Skinny girl, you need to put away some of your pay for emergencies. Do not inform anyone what amounts you save. Store some money aside, in case of a rainy day." She kept it simple, and it stuck. Life's detours can put us in unpredictable situations. Whether losing a job or heading to divorce court. These events impact the economic panorama. My mom's advice was intimidating but empowered me. We must be able to take care of ourselves financially. Relying on a man makes you vulnerable to financial ruin. There have been cases where men abandon their significant other leaving them destitute. Thank the justice system for divorce court. Whether married or single, a woman's slush fund should be on a list of best-kept secrets. Were it not for my private stash the situation could have been much harder. It takes about 21 days to establish a new habit. If we start by setting aside $10, $20 or $50 per paycheck, the habit becomes second nature. Everyone has a different budget to work with, my suggestion is an auto-savings deduction of an amount you can afford. It can be as little or as much as you can afford. It is not mandatory to sacrifice life's basic necessities. If in doubt, do your math. Select a random amount you are able to save from each paycheck. The average employee is paid twice per month. Try calculating the total bi-weekly savings amount by 12 months. Multiply that total number by years you've been with your partner. My relationship lasted 10 years – how long did yours last? Over time, the dollars add up. We are worth the investment in our own personal fund. I call it JICSH insurance (Just in case shit happens!). My daughter is now 16 years old. Last summer, she accepted her first summer job. The conversation when she received her paycheck started similarly to the one I had all those years ago with my own mother. There were a few additional topics during my conversation with her. Roth IRA and 401K were at the top of the list. Customize your financial plan to suit your lifestyle. It's crucial to educate yourself and your children.

In order to save more I would have to move to a place that was not only safe with good schools but reasonable. My sister found our new home in a town near her house. Distractions were everywhere, hindering me from focusing on solutions. Her specialty, God bless her soul! Lucky for me, she is a problem solver. I was obsessing about the problems lying ahead because I was in the center of a personal and financial mess. It is challenging to find your center in the midst of pandemonium. The charming Connecticut town was perfect for starting over. We fell in love with the cozy apartment when taken for a showing. A quaint townhouse on a quiet, tree-lined street, seven minutes from family. The move came within weeks of finding a place. Relocation to our neighboring state offered the opportunity for a clean slate. This was great stuff but at night when the world was sleeping – I was wide awake contemplating the reality unimagined. Over and over, I would ask myself, "Where would I draw strength from to get through?" The women around me were strong, independent but I didn't quite feel that way. I was afraid to disappoint my daughter. Fear of failure left me unable to keep a leveled head on most nights. Figuring out how to make the numbers work was the easy part. Learning to be emotionally independent was one of the battles for me. I wasn't ready to be on my own. New home, weekends alone without a clue of how to move into this new life. It was the price I was paying for living out my authenticity.

Flesh wounds were still fresh when acidic juices were splashed on it, exacerbating the internal bleeding. News arrived through the pipelines that my ex-husband had found a new partner. While the world stood still for me. Days, months passed leaving me behind in the race. It felt like a piece of glass slashed an aorta. My heart stopped momentarily, oxygen cut short. Have you ever felt a physical heartbreak? In the same instant, the phone rings—my daughter calling to check on me. Blood rushed back into my veins. Fury held back for the length of our call. An old set of dishes in my kitchen became clay targets used in a personal version of skeet shooting. Slow release of some of the madness brewing since the divorce began. His new courtship set off landmines in my brain. He was rebuilding the life I wanted with our daughter on Saturdays and Sundays. Meanwhile, my struggle to adjust to the new arrangement was never-ending. At least it felt that way for me.

A current life came with plenty of freedom, energy and buoyancy. But I still didn't know how to use it efficiently to shape my best self. I was secretly acrimonious, not successfully finding healthy outlets for release. It's easy to relinquish your power to vices while searching for relief. We live in an overmedicated society with access to all types of sedatives. A complete medicine cabinet available to escape reality and soften pain. Sex, pills, drugs, alcohol is all out there at our fingertips. We constantly need to remind ourselves that there are alternatives to avoid a path to self-destruction. The lesser of all evils for many females – Pinot. There is one for every palate – Pinot Grigio, Gris or Noir. On a whim, we'll shop around for its distant cousin Rose, Chardonnay and Sauvignon Blanc. Liquid lunches, dinners and any free hours in between. Surely, many of you have your own guilty pleasures. We all have a hidden armoire with some vice. Mine got me through many nights when the silence was deafening. The temporary state of insanity was short-lived. Ultimately, too expensive - physically, mentally and monetarily. Besides, not worth those hangovers at your desk the next morning.

Honestly, I didn't know what to do with myself. I began exploring every means to get clarity. In dire need to find peace, I took to reading. It eased some of my insomnia. I read all types of books but could not focus on any of them. Initially, I stayed out of the self-help section. Utterly ridiculous move since obviously, I required some assistance. I think there is an unfair stigma transferred from television and movies to real life. A portrayal of the desperate soul in the motivational books section is vastly exaggerated. We all need some assistance coping whether it's through conversation, reading or physical activity. Furious with the world and no plan of attack was mentally crushing. One night while surfing the web, I let myself imagine the possibilities. I wandered into Expedia.com. I had been reading *Eat, Pray, Love* that week. It came to me to buy a long weekend trip to Yellowstone National Park. If you have read this lovely book, you will understand my logic. The main character in the book takes a trip around the world hoping to find herself after a recent divorce. Sound familiar? It was a spur of the moment decision that lubricated the wheels of an old Corvette. I had lived for everyone else for so long. There was a strong will to live out my desires and do what made me happy. Or maybe, it was my way to start taking control back. Did I have the funds to make the trip? Not necessarily, but in that moment nothing was more important than what I needed. Unsure of how long this moment of fire would last, I went ahead and confirmed my flight itinerary. The next morning, I jumped on a flight to Billings, Montana with a connection in Denver. It sounds insane and trust me – I thought I had lost a marble or two. But the rush that came from making that one decision for myself had me spinning from the exhilaration! Fear was no longer a factor, it had the opposite effect. It made me want to live a daring and uncensored adventure. No expectations or concrete plans of what I would do when I landed in new territory. The past decade was full of schedules, dates on a calendar and fulfilling everyone else's needs. It was now time for me.

Montana was a spiritual and educational experience. I had never traveled alone. Ironically, I did not feel lonely during my travels. Being at home had the opposite effect. Residents and tourists were welcoming during the trip. Encountering humble and friendly folks made the experience rather pleasant. While the trek from New York City was long, it was worth the adventure. Nature all around me was breathtaking to see. Dressed in magnificent glory of pure beauty and peace. I saw Old Faithful, Bison, Black Bears, waterfalls and limitless acres of forest. Up until that point, I'd been going through so much but something interesting happened during my travels.

I was able to see past my troubles to understand how insignificant my worries were compared to the life thriving around me. Imagine the relief of coming up for air after holding your breath underwater for a few minutes. Divorce feels like a crash and burn but we have the capability to rise from the ashes if we allow ourselves. It was a short trip, enough days to regroup. The change of scenery gave me a burst of energy en route to a new perspective. Not for a moment did I fool myself into thinking the weekend away would wash away everything that was going on inside me. It provided a small break to reflect on some of the things I was feeling that weekend. Serving as a mental Post-It that there are happy people out there. Not every day, all day, but there are moments of joy for many of us.

On the return home, I jotted down a number of things I wanted to try but was too intimidated to do. A reintroduction to society was being summoned. Hiding in a cocoon forever was not an option. My daughter enjoyed weekends with her dad. I refused to take that away from her out of spite. Turn the other cheek as they say. Priorities shifted once he left home. I made a list of books to read. Unfortunately, I wasn't left with the mental energy for reading between work, motherhood and the mind racing at night. Constantly exhausted without relief in sight. I read an article about how exercise releases endorphins. The chemicals help one feel good, God knows I needed some of that! I signed up for a gym membership at the closest gym. Each day, I made it there for at least an hour to exercise. For my birthday, I received a set of private training sessions from my sister. I became obsessed with the gym but my eating habits suffered. Stress caused by the process was troublesome leaving me without appetite. The last thing on my mind was having three meals a day, so I would skip a couple. Losing weight was inevitable, I was working out heavily. My food intake was just enough to get me by, not the smartest nutrition plan. Unable to keep up the pace of everything, I slowed down at the gym.

I walked into the gym one weekday morning. The receptionist stared at me with concern. She checked my ID, frowned and asked "Ms. Bodden, are you feeling ok? You have lost an alarming amount of weight since you joined last month."

I responded with a smile "Yes, all good. Dealing with a lot of stress but thank you." When I got back home, I walked into my room. As I stood in front of the floor length mirror, I saw my collar bones protrude out of my v-neck t-shirt. I took a hard look at the woman in front of me. Dark circles around my eyes, a reflection of nights of insomnia. Pale, dry lips showing dehydration of a body that was starving of attention. This was not who I wanted my daughter to see. There had to be a way out of Oz. I continued looking for outlets to pull me out of this mental state where the witches and flying monkeys were attacking my well-being.

The next few weeks would be routine while I found other ways to release the demons. I thought a lot about my mom during my first several years after dad was out of the house. I recall music being played at home consistently. Although, sad to see my father go after his string of indiscretions, she didn't show as much anguish as I did during my breakup. Maybe, she suffered so much during the marriage it drained it all out of her. Letting go of a toxic relationship can do wonders or she found an outlet to purge. She dedicated herself to taking care of us. Her greatest joys were her kids and music. She'd spend all day listening to Kenny G and Whitney Houston while singing at top of her lungs to her favorite tunes. I wondered if music was her therapy. Studies have shown music can help improve your mood, energy level, and memory. It doesn't seem like a farfetched concept if you think about how many episodes of karaoke you've had in your car or shower after a crap day. Our playlists tend to coincide with how we are feeling at any given time. In my case, it was my way of venting aggression. I lived, breathed and ate songs that liberated me. The ultimate wish was getting my power back. The soundtrack to my ordeal went something like this:

1. "Numb" by Linkin Park
2. "Bring Me to Life" and "My Heart is Broken" by Evanescense
3. "Comfortably Numb" by Pink Floyd
4. "So What" by Pink

5. "Survivor" by Destiny's Child
6. "Salute" and "It's Not Right, but It's Okay" by Whitney Houston
7. "Deuces" by Chris Brown
8. "Hush Hush; Hush Hush" by The Pussycat Dolls
9. "Set Fire to the Rain" and "Rolling in the Deep" by Adele
10. "Back to Black" by Amy Winehouse
11. "Before He Cheats" by Carrie Underwood
12. "Fighter" by Christina Aguilera
13. "Superwoman" by Alicia Keys
14. "Grace of God" by Katy Perry

Incredibly, I was able to survive without playing the infamous Gloria Gaynor song we all know and love. I used music as a tool to empower me helping me draw strength and a pinch of boldness to get to the next day. People can drown in a pool of emotions. My vicious emotional rollercoaster was the ride that would not end. Denial was slowly subsiding. Feet firmly planted on the ground giving me a reality check. The picture in front of me was settling into my mind. My body became engulfed in anger producing moments of uncontrollable physical tremors. Most accurate way to describe the emotion? Similar to a cyclone ripping the roof off your home and simultaneously setting of the largest fault ever seen underground.

My world collapsed. I re-examined choices up to this stage. My ex-husband started a new storyline. I was returning to an old one from a decade ago. There were moments that dragged me through the mud. I picked myself up by the bootstraps knowing the misery would not last a thousand years. Repeatedly, I ignored the intensity felt deep within hoping it would go away. It did not disappear on its own. My temporary solution was to place a Band-Aid on the wound repeatedly and apply an anesthetic. I was upset he was able to get on with his life. Getting even with him crossed my mind on certain days. What stopped me from looking for ways to cause harm? There was an ounce of pride preventing me from stooping too low. I loved him and our daughter even more. Revenge would have added pessimism to an already awful situation that could have brought our daughter distress. Giving myself permission to lash out risking any sort of damage was not a viable option for me. Attempts at finding other ways to release was a good start for recovery of a broken heart. Listening to music improves mood, significantly assists with workouts to burn calories. It all leads to perking up your mental energy. The angry stage of grief creates an imbalance sending the most Zen person to spiral into unknown territory. Everyone is capable of behaving badly. We have a responsibility to manage our thoughts and actions in the best possible manner. This requires redirecting anger in ways that will aid to safely release it.

We Almost Had It All, Only If...
(BARGAINING)

Divorce forced me to ask myself questions on just about everything. Second-guessing my world, faith, and beliefs. I trusted love would win when it is real. The dissolution of the marriage put that ideal to rest. I'm not overly religious but I have conviction in a greater being. On the way home from the office, I stopped at my favorite church in the city. I found a pew to sit quietly with my thoughts. St. Patrick's Cathedral is masterful in size and presence. It is estimated that over a million candles are lit in prayer every year. The number of visitors walking into the church is at least double that number. I arrived a touch confused about what I was looking for that day. Was I seeking something to believe in, again? Have you ever felt lost and asked "Why?" or "What if you would have made a different decision? Would it have changed the outcome?" Our lives could have been perfect were it not for this one mishap. Is this really true? I built a career out of fooling myself ignoring reality when convenient. Finally, when I stood in front of the mirror of truth, the glass shattered into the million lies I had been telling myself.

As women, we experience pressure from society, work, family to fit a label or mold. We spend much of our tender years observing the older generations. Our mothers sacrificed their dreams to allow room for family. Since then, roles played inside and outside the home have notably changed society. Thanks to modern medicine and a longer lifespan we are waiting later in life to bear children. This is a meaningful reversal from what our mothers and grandmothers experienced. Unfortunately, the weight of the roles we are "supposed to" play continues. Invisible rules imposed by others can periodically force us to conform to lives that don't necessarily make us happy. We are guilted into maintaining a façade, so we do not stray on the path less traveled. Our jobs as caretakers require that we put others first. When we don't, it can cause chaos affecting all parties. I felt responsible for my family's happiness in every area. As Mrs. Fixer Upper, it was up to me to make life better for my loved ones. While skipping down the yellow brick road, I abandoned a critical piece of the journey. I lost myself. This neglect produced a crack in the foundation. Efforts to cover up the holes that popped up were useless after figuring out there were too many to spackle.

Was there an option to repair what had been broken? Would I be able to return to sacrificing my identity to fulfill the needs of this other person? It all sounded insane and unsustainable at that point. The idea I could give up my happiness to hand it to someone else was no longer on the agenda. How could I make anyone happy if I was not feeling it for myself? All scenarios played in my head but none were feasible. The unraveling of life was as unstoppable as a runaway train.

I was wrapped up in a blanket of guilt during this period. Parts of me wondered did I deserve this pain? Should I had done anything differently could I have kept the family together? But returning to a damaged relationship was not an option. What could I do to eliminate the ill feelings I had ingested? A tug of war between regret and doubt left nothing to barter. I owed myself to come to terms with the mess. Millions of others were in the same predicament because love is not always enough. Breakups occur to the most seemingly perfect couples.

Subsequently, months after, the remorse paused. A stillness set into my world. Exhaustion could have been the culprit. The period offered time of reflection on what was happening. A marriage – the longest relationship of my adulthood – was dead. I was entering a metamorphosis. The woman of the past decade was shedding dead weight. Even if I wanted to regress, the power of "Me" was stronger. No longer would I be able to hold back the empowerment I was feeling from dropping layers of insecurity, self-doubt, and guilt. A clarity was beginning to shine through to the external world. Confronting the woman I was meant to become was inevitable.

Tunnel of Darkness, My Cave
(DEPRESSION)

We all have our share of problems. Some more than others but everyone has blunders on life's resume. I spent a great deal of energy trying to wrap the events that took take place in a neat little package but it was far from what I was living. I'm not sure if my disposition came from a need to be perceived as perfect or out of a desire to have a different outcome than my parents. Either way, unrealistic expectations were definitely present in my relationship. I swept my dirt under the rug to paint a pretty picture. Human beings are complicated, life is complex. We do the best we can, ironing out kinks along the way. Looking back, my biggest mistake was ignoring my gut when it told me something was off. The weeks and months following our acknowledgment the marriage was done were the worst. I think the admission of failure was as detrimental as the events leading up to it. I was certain it was over. Mourning set in making me feel anxiety and terrible. The despair added the weight of boulders on my feet. It became difficult to manage my everyday. It was a struggle to get myself up despite having every reason to do it. I should have been relieved to close a chapter. Instead, my body was half-alive. The strength of 1000 warriors laid on my shoulders hindering me from taking a step towards the future. My spirit was broken from the notion of defeat. I loved him but had to give him up because I was learning self-love. I was growing to value myself more than a man. A win that cost everyone unhappiness, short term.

Saturdays and Sundays were rough during divorce. We agreed to share custody of our daughter which meant dividing time between homes. My ex-husband went away one weekend leaving her home with me. I was elated to have her but could barely crawl out of bed.

The blackout curtains had not been drawn all day. It was a Saturday morning around 11:00 am when she stepped into my room. My precious baby girl was about 6-years old, yet wise beyond her years. Standing in front of my bed, she looks at me and says "Mommy you've been in bed all morning, can you get out of your cave? I'm hungry. When will you get out of bed? When can we open the curtains and let sunlight into your bedroom." She saw right through me that day. At that moment, I knew immediately I couldn't fight this alone. It was a duty and responsibility to start the healing for her sake. I made one call on Monday morning to a therapist referred to me by a friend.

The appointment with the therapist came sooner than expected. She had a cancellation bringing me into her office the following morning. Unsure of what the session would bring to my day, I took a personal day from work. I walked into the office feeling immediate comfort by the surroundings. It was as if I walked into a familiar space, like a friend's living room. Her grayish hair was pulled back, drawing attention to her light green eyes. She inspired warmth and trust. There was an immediate connection that gave me ease to speak to her openly. Her voice was soft and soothing to me. One of the primary questions after her introduction "Why are you here today?" I was glad to vent about my crazy to the complete stranger not there to judge me – just listen. Once done, she must have had an idea of where I was coming from because she asked an interesting question. She directed her eyes to me and said "If you had to choose one of these two things to have the best life. Which would you prefer to have - security or your freedom?" The question demanded some consideration but I was certain that most of my life, I sought a sense of security from being in a relationship. For as long as I could remember, I got my self-worth and feeling of protection from partners, it was my norm. She suggested I save the response to write in a journal. Afterward, commenting that she'd ask the same question again at a later date.

A decision to seek guidance was best because the blues weren't going away. The sorrow began affecting every aspect of my life from the way I interacted with people to how I managed my every day. I felt things would never improve. I began treating myself like I didn't deserve better because I had failed at my marriage, leaving my daughter a victim of a broken home. Depression leaves you in a state of sadness and hopelessness. Loss resulting from death or divorce can trigger the temporary condition. I started with the blues but things progressively worsened with my alienation from others. Excruciating heartache had forced me to build a wall around me. I retreated to loneliness that was as painful as it was comforting. I shut myself down, producing that numbing effect that was all too familiar.

The goal in my mind was to protect myself from vulnerability. I didn't count on it partially shutting down emotions to avoid pain. I kept joy out because I was afraid to have it and lose it again. Truth is, real courage comes from being vulnerable. Feeling the emotions we are designed to experience. I will not mislead you into thinking a few sessions led to an epiphany. A month or two of therapy did not suffice. Due to the different variables that can affect treatment, it's essential to have patience with the process and yourself. It is also helpful to have a connection with the person on the other side of the couch. The success of therapy relies on a number of factors. There is nothing easy about opening up to someone. The idea of spitting out gory details of your deepest, darkest thoughts is terrifying. It can scare the heck out of any of us! Everyone has moments they stream their personal trajectory in their minds. Replaying chapters out loud of how we have screwed ourselves or someone else is a lousy game. Throw in childhood drama into the mix, it can all look very distorted. It's a doozy! Much digging required that not everyone is prepared to do, nevertheless, worth it? Absolutely for some – me included. It took years to make amends with myself.

The depressive state was draining me. Bless my sisters for kicking my butt when I needed it! Several components went into making small improvements on my way to a better place. There's a stigma that comes with divorce. Two things to keep in mind, what you are going through is normal. We do not expect to separate when getting married but it happens for a bunch of reasons. Going through a rough patch and getting down about what you have been through is nothing to be shameful of, almost half of all marriages end in divorce court. Sadly, the statistics are there and continue to shift in minor increments. The second thought to keep at the forefront, despite life placing boulders in your trail. You are going to find your way around the mountain.

My bout with depression was scary, debilitating to a degree. So much, it had me anxiously waiting for my weekly therapy sessions. Our meetings became an outlet to release negative energy. Few and far, days in between I felt hope that I'd come out of the hot mess. I held on to the love of my daughter. Knowing she needed me gave me a reason to love myself on the bad days. Approximately eight months into my sessions, the therapist asked if I wanted to try an antidepressant to help me in the interim. Research proved valuable after considering the options. I took a brutal look at the facts in order to come to a decision that would most benefit my long term mental health. Having a bad reaction while on contraception lead me to be careful of medications in general. Determining whether or not to try antidepressants as a short term measure to deal was a brain-teaser. I asked myself three questions:

1. **Did I pose a danger to myself or others?** Instinctively, I knew this was not the case.
2. **Was the pain of depression so unbearable that it would hinder**

me from fulfilling responsibilities at home or work? Surely, I was sad but fully capable of taking care of baby girl. My priorities were being a mom and provider. Two roles, I couldn't afford to jeopardize no matter how much misery a broken heart was bringing me.

3. **In my heart-of-hearts, did I feel that if I didn't take those meds, I wouldn't get better?** Not the case, either.

That same week while in conversation with my sister, I unloaded my dilemma along with another tearful story. I repeatedly talked about how unsuccessful my attempts at marriage had been and how love got me to my present misfortune. Maybe she was tired of seeing me in misery, and so she offered tough love. One simple but powerful statement resonated with me. It never quite left me. Her words amplified like a blow horn to my ear "You have the power to stop this, YOU need to make the choice to stop being the victim!" she said with candor. During the following appointment, I expressed the decision to turn down meds choosing to stick to therapy. I shared the details of my conversation with my sister that week. It was an "IT" moment. The turning point when the power shifted back to me. The true work began there. It took every ounce of will to dig myself out of the grave.

Despite the mountain of struggles, I consider myself lucky. I battled a round of depression due to this life-changing event named divorce. There are those who have to continuously fight with mental illness. According to National Institute of Mental Health in 2017, over 16.1 million people were affected by Major Depressive Disorder (MDD). MDD is more prevalent in women than men. The rate of adults receiving medical care for the disorder is a mere 61.7%, not shocking if your eyes are open to the current mental health crisis in the United States. Many lack the support or resources needed to manage their health. Therapy helped me understand that I had an integral part in the healing process. The therapist gave me tools to cope with my ordeal while learning to sort through the emotions in a healthy manner. This called for a long time of self-examination exploring what makes me tick. I was forced to dig deep to the core to figure out who I was and how I contributed to the problem. Most of all, I needed to decide who I wanted to be from now on. It was a pivotal moment if I wanted to bring the essence of who I was to the forefront. Doing so would provide a real sense of freedom.

Ticks We Need to Get to Know and Learn to Live With

How do you start figuring out what makes you tick? Why is it important to know? There are dozens of ways we use a form of identity. You have a passport, driver's license, fingerprints, and retina scan. The modern world has ample forms of identifying who we are. But do you know who you are? This undertaking helped me realize that knowing who I am is a key component to finding real happiness.

I had no idea where to begin but these questions can initiate the task:

1. Do you know what your gifts are or what you are good at? It should be easy but an abundance of people don't know their talents. They learn a skill or job and roll with it. It's easy to get lost in others forgetting what you bring to the table. Take pause. Awareness of the value you add is necessary for personal growth.
2. Why are you where you are? Have you followed someone else's dream? Were you told to follow a path by a parent or husband? Did any particular challenges force you to shy away from what you have been wanting to do? Are you standing up for what you want? Are you content with the life you're living and what you are doing? If not, are you doing something about it?
3. Are you living the life you desire according to what you believe?

Have you behaved in a manner that you are proud of and sticking to your principles?
4. Do you know what your passion is? Are you living with purpose? Do you live a life that reflects truth?

These are tough questions which have taken years for me to answer. Everyone is a work in progress. When I began to ask myself these questions new doors opened. Once it set off, nuggets of wisdom were found along the way clearing a path. Living in true-self form unleashes your truths as a woman and human being. Those answers held the key to genuine happiness. In theory, the task is not too hard? Just be yourself. Accept who you are as a whole, flaws and all. The end result will be joy but the work must be done. Keep a journal to write your thoughts. It might be easiest to sit in a quiet space alone to jot down what you are thinking. The mind will try to chase out thoughts you aren't prepared to see. You can drown the noise. Silence the negativity long enough to let emotions come together with your mind.

The fear that followed me around was hard to shake. I knew finding out what made me tick would put me face to face with some things I did not like about myself. Unfortunately, one of the major issues we have is living in our own skin. Many of us prefer to use a mask to help hide our imperfections. It's no walk in the park to let people on the outside see the cracks we carry inside. It makes us vulnerable and open to criticism. You must understand that mistakes or failures do not define us. It's OK to feel sad, angry or hurt and others to see the imperfection of our lives. Once a marriage or any relationship ends, you are in your right to mourn for however long it takes to heal. Own your pain, process it and keep moving forward. Keep in mind, self-care is part of the way to crawling out of the misery.

Circumstances and thresholds for pain vary from person to person, so don't feel pressure to be done with it on anyone else's timetable. I don't ever want the journey of grief to sound like a walk in the park. It's not. Undoubtedly, whether it's the depression itself or therapy – both will be challenging. But you can overcome pain. The most profound and miserable stage for me was the depression. It was filled with unimaginable hurt that can solely be understood by those who have lived in the darkness of the cave it puts us in. However, help is available to sufferers who seek it. There are moments during any traumatic event where you just need an ear. Opening a line of communication with someone can make a world of difference. Help is available to everyone. If the weight on your shoulders is too heavy, let someone help you carry the load. Seek guidance from family members, friends, spiritual mentor or therapist.

We get hit hard with problems throughout our lives. The punches come rolling, a slew of them below the belt. The power of a jab can take the air out of our lungs. Sufficient blows, and we will feel defeated. Assuming, we in some way deserve it. The tiredness of the situation will wear you down to believe things won't get better. Don't despair, the human spirit is a great force. You can put your life back together again brick by brick. Choose yourself every day. The work will pay off.

No More Monsters!
(ACCEPTANCE)

Acceptance is the last stage of the grieving period. It's the part of the process where you bring yourself back to the reality of your relationship. The point where you come to terms with the event taking place. The relief felt from the awakening was liberating. There are setbacks because any of these stages can return to haunt you. It's to your benefit to comprehend that everyone experiences grief their own way. Some stages will be brief while others hit the repeat button. Don't feel discouraged if the grief comes back for you. Falling back into a bad groove is understandable. The life altering event is going to turn you inside out but fight the negativity. Don't let it swallow you because there is much to live after a breakup. The love is limitless once you find it within yourself.

This part of your tale has ended but another chapter is beginning! Or so I thought, there was still a dim light that would not let me come full circle. Completely distraught at the onset of the breakup. I had a beaten spirit crushed by love's disillusionment with little or no hope of feeling whole again. Best way to describe my state is to compare it to a horse with a broken spirit. Before a horse is broke, it is put through training that calls for disciplining by dominance using fear and pain. The term comes from the old days when the claim is cowboys would actually break a horse's spirit to teach them to be ridden. I was that horse, my soul was shattered. The stages of grief are exhausting. I was not sure who I was or where I was headed. I was refusing any type closeness or intimacy to protect myself from hurt. The emotional window was closed. The embarrassment of a failed marriage and aching heart had me spinning out of control. My assumption that the inability to keep the family together was a failure crushed me. The shame of failing at giving my daughter a blissful home was highly upsetting, as it can be for most women. A decision to continue therapy was obvious. I knew it would demand a commitment to stick to every appointment. Accepting the challenge to be deliberately truthful was brutal. Telling my story in its entirety - good, bad and ugly which is never pretty.

Reading Brenee Brown's "The Gifts of Imperfection" had a strong impact on me. The book was recommended by my therapist during one of our early sessions. Her written word accompanies me at various moments of life. The book explains how it's ok to be vulnerable, afraid and to make mistakes. She writes about about vulnerability, courage, authenticity, and shame. None of these things makes you imperfect or less worthy. To the contrary, her message was "YOU are enough, as you are" . The bravery is in living your truth. The text gave me a sense of belonging which was a godsend throughout the initial part of therapy. I wasn't alone feeling this way. It gave me a sense of normalcy to feel that being imperfect didn't take away from the woman I was.

One of the most difficult aspects of divorce grief is accepting defeat. Losing a love as a result of the battle you've endured. There is a mountain of pressure on women to be everything to everyone. This can lead to setting unrealistic expectations for ourselves by thinking we can be the perfect wife, mother, and career professional. In the same breath, willing to give up part or all of you are to make sure we secure the sacred image. Perfection is not attainable but we continue to aspire to the throne. While managing the various roles, we should try to understand that mistakes will be made. It is fact of life. Faux-pas do not in any way diminish self-worth. Whether working from home or office, it is a juggling act to maintain it all in balance. Accepting the finality requires admission that things are not functioning. It serves no good purpose to view it as a failure which I believe a bunch of us do. Spending endless amounts of time trying to fit a mold or make others happy. It takes plenty of work to *play perfect*. Funny thing, I was far from it. I recall being in the ladies room at work one day. A colleague several years older than myself approached me while I was primping in front of the mirror. She stared at me momentarily.

"How do you do it? You always look so perfect. Each hair in place," she said with a grin.

"Oh, thank you. You are too sweet. That's very nice of you to say." I responded quite graciously not to lead her to think there was conceit on my part.

At that moment, her comment had me basking in the glory of a win. The idea that someone perceived me as flawless meant my hard work was paying off. Granted, it was 10 seconds of glee, short-lived. When she walked out and the moment was over, a light bulb went off in my head. How many people shared her sentiment? Why was it important that people have this perception of me? The pressure I'd been carrying was ridiculous and unfair. What good did it do to paint a artful masterpiece on the outside if it was not genuine? I created such an illusion. Imagine the annihilation of coming clean about the breakup while everyone is seeing it unfold? It is a spotlight that I did not want on my life. During acceptance, I finally let go. In no way does it mean the the hurt stopped. Giving up the dream of perfection allowed me to own who I was, and get forgiveness. It was one of the hardest things to do. We can be our own worst critic. But regardless of the reason or reasons for the breakup, you will have to find absolution. This was a big step putting me on a path of true acceptance.

Through therapy, I learned to own my mistakes. Understand that my choices didn't make me a bad person. Trusting the process encouraged a personal evolution as it took me through several stages towards becoming my best self. I figured out that self-respect was worth fighting for intently. I was entitled to demand more of myself and others. If the marriage was not allowing me the freedom to find my authentic self then it was not right for me. There should never be shame in being yourself. It was an epic moment, when the chains broke off. Noticing that locking myself into a confined role of wife and mother was harming to me. It no longer felt OK to sacrifice my identity for the sake of others. The offering was not equal the cost of admission. The lessons of divorce were invaluable as they introduced me to meet the woman I am today. The grief lasted a few years for me. There is no specific deadline to "get over it" as they say.

Grief is dark and lonely, makes it hard to see the light. I couldn't see any brightness at the end of the tunnel. On the day of my breakthrough, I recall leaving the therapist's office and looking up at a blue sky. I saw color – it was the bluest sky you've ever seen. I texted her, "Thank you. For the first time in a while, I see in color." I felt freedom, relief, and love for myself. The therapist, asked the same question that she did on the first day I walked into her office those few years before, "If you had to choose between having your freedom or security. Which would you choose today?" I feel alive. I'm free.

PART II
AWAKENING

My acceptance of the event initiated a purge of sorts. Most of us want what we want when we want it or fool ourselves into thinking we already have it, even if we do not.. On the basis of need, we force our hand even though the acquisition might not be in our best interest. If we look around, there are dozens of examples. There is the woman who just snatched a great job, and in an effort to impress new colleagues, she shows up to her first day with the newest Gucci bag or red bottom shoes. Then there's the guy who needs to purchase the best big screen television to have friends over on Super Bowl Sunday. We seek approval or nurturing from our parents, children, friends, or mate. Couples have been known to stay together to satisfy a need for comfort or security. Willing to risk authenticity in the name of preservation. We invest loads of energy while looking for the love of a lifetime. One person to share our dreams. You want to hold on with both tooth and nail but you won't win every battle.

My parents divorced when I was much older. The separation didn't have the same effects on my mom as mine had on me. Although, their love-hate relationship was not my experience. My ex-husband and I shared good love. It just wasn't the right type of love for me. Intuitively, from the beginning of our courtship, I knew deep down we weren't a great fit. The phrase "opposites attract" sounds exciting in theory, but it's a tough sell, now. Living on opposite ends of the pole with your partner can leave a lot of room for misinterpretation. It's not that you have to be twinsies, but interests and goals should align, organically. I spent a great deal of life thinking that the love and acceptance of a partner were necessary to make me whole. Make me happy. The skies were clear and blue on the day, I awakened. My eyes were finally wide open.

Growing up I read books or watched movies in which a character has an epiphany, awakening, or enlightening. It's a state of "clear consciousness" where you find a genuine connection to your true self. It's not a flash moment but a process you go through taking you to an unfamiliar level self-awareness. A natural or traumatic event usually triggers this during movie reels. Truth is, at the time, it all seemed like a fluffy concept. If asked about it today, I'd disagree with my younger self. Divorce took me to a cold, dark and lonely place inside my head. I was able to come full circle only after experiencing all the stages of grief. Once I made the choice to take an active part in my therapy things began to improve. The memory of the day I broke through the icy pond is as vivid as if it had happened yesterday.

It was a Saturday morning in June. Four years of therapy appointments later, I saw color in my canvas, again. Sunny skies adorned by white cumulus, cotton-like clouds. The trees were stuffed with vibrant green leaves. The patches at the nearby house were showing pink rosebuds blooming. I could not recall the last time since separation that I saw color. I'm not kidding you. Imagine living with black and white tv then seeing the same thing in color! On that day, I walked out feeling lighter. The sounds of summer and the feel of a warm breeze in my hair revived me. It was the moment I felt my soul return to my body. I was done existing and ready to reintegrate myself with the rest of the living.

There would be a long road ahead waiting for me. I knew the journey to the "Holy Grail" as Jen Sincero referred to it, was just beginning! I was in a place of positivity, yet complete happiness was still elusive. We spend a substantial amount of our lives searching for happiness with each of us having a different idea of what it means. I thought it was a place of bliss where I would arrive someday. This would be my daily happy place. Part of this scavenger hunt involved finding the perfect partner to share nirvana with me like the fairy tales we read about as children. Yes, insanely naïve, isn't it? Well, there is no prince and no castle but joy is found beyond disillusionment. Toward the end of therapy when things started taking shape, I had numerous questions for myself. One of the first things, I needed to do was figure out what made me happy.

On my own without a man or a child in my picture - Who Am I? I think we stop asking ourselves this question when we become mothers and wives. We do whatever is required to become the picture of superwoman. It's like looking for Wonder Woman on Paradise Island. There is no such place. What was next for me after coming out of the darkness of divorce? How to get back to work from a position of strength? There was a lot of work to be done. I wrote out more activities to try in attempting to regain my power. One of the things, I wished to do was read as much, as time allowed. Learn and re-educate myself on life by finding books by people, I admired. During this quest, which I'll discuss in detail later in the book, I read Jen Sincero's "You Are a Badass." In it, she makes a powerful statement that I carry in my back pocket: "Love yourself because it's the holy grail of happiness." Those are some of the strongest words you can pull together. I spent years giving my all to others. Thirsty for love and approval while neglecting to seek it within. I did not get the concept for much of my dating years impacting me personally and romantically.

My parents did the best they could with us. My mother was demanding and strict but loving. She had high expectations for me. Anything less than perfect would not do. It's what she knew to be right. Passing the baton down to me was counterproductive, it affected my self-esteem. Growing up it became my norm to feel, if I wasn't flawless, I wasn't complete. Carrying this boulder of pressure weighed heavily on me. Each mistake diminishing me to the point of feeling undeserving of good things. I could not anticipate how I'd get out from under the rubble I found myself under after two failed marriages. I was crushed but took away some valuable lessons. The rebuilding phase was part of a path to self-worth.

There is healing after the pain of any breakup. Today my ex-husband and his family along with myself all celebrate our daughter's successes together. We recently joined together to give her a Sweet 16 party which turned out to be memorable and emotional. Each one of us makes a contribution to making her life better. She feels the security of two loving families. Peacefully, she enjoys the benefits of a tribe that supports and works in unison to fortify her well-being. The process of making amends has taken years. Finally, bringing everyone to a place of peace where we take nothing for granted. She came from love, and we committed ourselves to raise her in that same nurturing circle. Setting aside differences was a decision made by both because our love for her is greater than anything. Not all couples are able to come through to the other side amicably or even, cordially. If it is possible, it's worth the effort because it improves the emotional and psychological wellness of everyone involved. We all have our battles to fight. I can now see the road ahead to the next set of challenges. I will confront whatever comes stronger and wiser.

Challenges fortify our lives in various ways. It became my mission to explore things that would help me continue to gain inner strength. Whether choosing to call this finding a purpose or being enlightened, one has to take action. The ability to take a step towards forgiveness and freedom after separation is progress. It's not a simple ask. I don't intend to minimize it, mainly when entangled in a web of emotions. Children can definitely add layers of complication. Their mental health is a priority for parents in turmoil. However, adults set the example and carry the family. Kids look to their parents for security and support. We have a responsibility to ourselves and to the children We must fight to be whole and stay present. This will help ensure you can take care of everyone that requires it, starting with yourself. If decay reaches the trunk of the family tree then things fall apart. Inevitably, the weakened state can deteriorate a relationship from the inside out. Nurture the mind, body and soul to restore mental health. Push forward. Take the bull by the horns because there is so much already in our realm that is out of our control. Begin the work to help rebuild your inner core. Hopefully, something on the following list will resonate with you to help jumpstart the ignition on your life. You are the driver on this one. Take the wheel.

Six Power Moves to Help Wake You after Divorce

Cherish Your Mental, Physical and Emotional Well-Being

Divorce is ever-changing. The stress from it can be devastating, turning your universe inside out and affecting your health. The Holmes And Rahe Scale (1967) also known as SSRS (Social Readjustment Rating Scale) is often used to pinpoint which groups of individuals could be at highest risk of getting sick as a result of stressors caused by high-level life-changing events. Would you be surprised to know divorce is ranked #2 on that list? Not surprising news if you have been through one. Death and imprisonment are runners up to the stress of a marital separation. The stressor threatens our physical, psychological and emotional well-being. It leads to illnesses such as chronic pain, obesity, diabetes, anxiety, and depression, just to name a few.

Pain took me through a whirlwind tunnel of emotions that affected stress levels. Separations, divorces, breakups are tricky depending on the situation of parties involved. There are a handful of amicable ones where partners act in accordance. Couples agree that the decision to part is best for everyone. Other breakups can turn volatile and angry when someone is left behind jealous or disappointed. The one leaving the party of two will likely feel a wrath.

When we talk about separation of any equity (money, children, house) things can get intensely problematic. Distress will take over every inch of your brain.

The breakup did a job on my body. Have you ever fallen asleep crying, barely making it through the night then eventually fall asleep to wake up, again in tears? I lost my appetite with barely any brawn to get myself going. Mustering up any bit of spark to rise up and get my daughter out the door for school then work on weekdays. Around the time divorce was hitting its peak point, I woke up to find my pillow full of hair. On average, women lose 50-100 strands of hair per day. My hair was falling out much more, alarming my senses. Over months, showers were my worst nightmare due to the amounts of hair in the bathtub. I cried incessantly about the hair loss but underneath it was also for myself.

During one of my weekly appointments, my hairdresser asked if things were ok. She told me not to freak out while I watched from the mirror as she brushed handfuls of long strands right out of my scalp. Witnessing the hair loss made more upset. The doctor recommended prenatal vitamins to strengthen my system. Biotin was all the rave, I would have tried anything to cure the hair loss. Unfortunately, I had a bad reaction and immediately stopped the supplement. It took about 6 months before I was able to recover from that episode. The depression, hair loss, weight loss, and lack of sleep consumed me. I was letting the mental and physical deterioration attack my body. Surely, you've had your own health battles during bad breakups or separations. I have been where you are and cannot say it enough – you must love yourself. Make your health a priority. Don't let stress beat you. Our mind is a powerful tool we can use to help or hurt our bodies. Accept the support of loved ones to get through this time. The pain of defeat can fool you into social isolation. It is prone to create a lonely world inside your soul, but you can surpass the terrible effects brought on by the ordeal. You are a product of your thoughts. Treat your brain like a muscle, exercise it. Feed it good information to promote the best health. The physical being follows suit. We get one body, treat it like a temple.

Yvette Bodden

Choose You

Generally, nature tugs at women's nurturing side. We try to care for loved ones even if it requires our needs take a backseat temporarily. There is almost an innate aspect for our gender to tend to others. When we go against the will to give unselfishly, guilt can be all too consuming but we push it down for the sake of those we love. I'm no exception, in fact, I'm an example of this quality. Since the divorce, I have had to reprogram much of my thinking. I grew up seeing my mother do the cooking, cleaning and just about everything for us. Assuming it was the right way of doing things, I fell in the same routine in my own world. But we should try to be a little selfish without feeling we are letting anyone down. In an effort to do just that, each year around my birthday, I organize special events to celebrate life. A tour of North Fork Winery with girlfriends, fancy dinners and spa days. One year, the celebration took a few of us to a beautiful beach on Puerto Rico. Another birthday took me to Las Vegas hosting a couple fun-filled nights. Moments of joy to cherish, keeping in my memory bank to recall now and then. I make it my business to treat myself because it's essential to maintaining my sanity. I organize the annual event way in advance to ensure nothing falls through the cracks including my budget. I gave birth to the idea after the separation. During my marriage, we celebrated as a family. Moments treasured, although privately it didn't feel like my day. If it was my birthday, I alone should choose how to spend it. Not usually the way the day goes down. How many girlfriends, wives, mothers dream about a day to do nothing? How often have we wished someone would wait on our every whim? Does it happen sporadically? Most definitely. A handful of times, maybe. If your partner makes it happen, great! Piece of advice for you, if he does, take him and run. You will never find me complaining about my birthdays, Mother's Day or any celebrations while married because they were all made to be special. It is not in our DNA to give ourselves permission to be selfish. I have realized how unhealthy it is to carry the guilt of wanting more. No longer do I wait for birthdays to do something nice for myself. A balance between the giving and receiving does not mean having to compromise your needs. That won't get you equilibrium. Do things that make you feel good. Don't feel like you have to say yes to everything and everyone. Sometimes, it will mean going against the grain or disappointing people. Pleasing an entire audience is not practical. I choose me every day after understanding that my happiness is as important as anyone else's - probably moreso. All in moderation, of course. Balance is the key to everything.

Yvette Bodden

Self-Examination
"The unexamined life is not worth living." – Socrates

There are those who walk their path without purpose while others are constantly looking for reason. I never asked myself the real questions as I did post-divorce. It is difficult to be brutally honest with oneself. I wasn't prepared to hear my truths. However, set out to go on a mission of self-improvement by using the lessons, I forged an introspection of sorts. The task of connecting the dots opened the door to authenticity. Much of it meant having to accept bad decisions made on my part. Taking responsibility for mistakes can be challenging. There was so much uncertainty moving ahead. How did I arrive at this crossroad? What did I stand for? I had been sailing along missing a compass or map. I took whatever was swung my way because it was easier than going after what I wanted or deserved. There is risk when asking for what we need. There is a chance of rejection which is something I feared terribly, as many of us do. One of the many discoveries made along the journey was that my identity was tied to a relationship. It took a wake up call to show me I was giving more than taking while trying to bind my worth to a man. Deconstructing all this was a huge undertaking. I was facing my ugly. Talk about turning a blind eye. Red flags were signaling me all along. I kept my eyes closed to the waving banners. We make the choice whether or not to overlook danger. Our gut, the inner voice tugging at us when we're not doing right, does not ignore facts. Paying close attention to the warnings can save you from future heartbreak.

Mistakes do not have to define you, so live fearlessly. Look within for answers to the real you. Be bold and dare to seek truth. Take a self inventory to get to know the woman in the mirror. In order to be yourself - you must first, find yourself. This is crucial. Once you have those answers, jot down one small goal for yourself with a date of completion. Baby steps as you get stronger. Every goal set and achieved will help you gain confidence. You can do this!

Find Your Energy Source - Outlet

Divorce has the ability to drain a person's or family's emotional and physical health. For the person fighting this heartbreaking battle, it can knock the wind out of you. It is key to find a source to recharge while searching for answers and picking up the pieces from the life-changing event. As I said earlier, the first place I looked to regain energy was the local gym. Exercise releases endorphins which sets off signals in your brain that help relieve pain. Simultaneously, these chemicals can set off happy feelings in our bodies. Staying active in any way helps regenerate. Take walks, run or utilize 10 minutes a day to get the motor running. It's a good time to experiment with all the different ways one can absorb positive movement. Create a playlist with music that will uplift you. Tunes that make you want to shake it up - dance! Dancing is another great way to promote euphoria. Although dancing won't wash away worries, it can give you a temporary state of elation. Every little step advances the process.

During this stage, I couldn't find adequate ways to release. The gym held my attention for as long as I could pay the monthly dues. Newly single and with a child, adding a bill to my monthly budget was not a long term option. I needed an activity I could do when the funds allowed without committing to contracts. One day during my morning reading, I came across an article about boxing. The sport is beneficial to the body and the mind. Body movements create challenges for our muscles as well as our brain. Focus is required which does two things for us. First, it can take you out of the moment into a world that is all about you. Encountering the inner fighter as you release stress to power back the machine. Secondly, constant learning of various offensive and defensive moves would keep anyone on their toes. Added benefits include workouts that can potentially burn a substantial amount of calories and strengthen upper and lower body muscles. The gym was a good source to get motivated again. Boxing turned out to be the best fit for me. It got me in the zone, a go-to spot to lose myself. I was willing to try it all to drop the feeling of defeat that haunted me for so long. The need to feel alive again was palpable. I wanted to be resuscitated, stopping at nothing to get those paddles working at my heart. Making the connection between mind, body and soul shocked my system like an electric current. If you can find an outlet that provides a similar sensation, you have found your personal energy source. The activity has centered me, strengthening my mental and physical core. It's paid off in self-awareness and renewed energy, bringing a sense of tranquility to my life.

Of course, boxing is not for everyone. I would advise against investing in an activity that does not interest you. The exercise is to seek diversion that calls your attention. Stay open to the possibilities. You might be surprised to discover something you never thought about doing. Heartbreak can leave anyone in bad shape but human beings are resilient. We have the power to change things within our control. Our mind and bodies get used to whatever we feed it. Plug yourself into a field of positivity by supplying it with goodness. The other thing to do is laugh out loud. Laughter has numerous benefits – among them, they also releasing endorphins and lower stress hormones. These two factors alone can improve well-being, making things better. Mild relief can be delivered from the simplest of activities, such as watching a funny movie or laughing at a silly joke. This power move has shown me the importance of creating my own fountain of energy so I can be a solid source of support for my loved ones. I can't be strong for them if I don't show up for myself.

See the Beauty in Who You Are

Relationships fail for a variety of reasons. The main component in the dismantling of mine was trying to build the marriage on the shoulders of my roles as caretaker. I neglected the woman within. I lost myself on the way to making a happy home. We crack our heads trying to figure out who we are, some of us never quite solve the puzzle. There is power in having conviction in your beliefs and values. Setting personal limits and knowing what brings you joy without surrendering or selling out to the masses is work. Endless challenges exist in reaching a true sense of self. If you're fortunate enough to meet your truth be prepared for extra rounds. The gloves don't come off when you find authenticity. The exercise continues even after arriving at this realization. The selection of the right partner to share your life adds a layer of complexity. Love means compromise, right? Who sets boundaries in these negotiations? Who writes the rules? Is it fair to ask anyone to give up their identity, forcing assimilation in a relationship whether married or not? Why would you be willing to hand over the power of YOU? I did, and personally, it cost me. I walked into my marriage with barely an idea of who I was. It provided an opportunity for a bigger personality to swallow me whole. Believing it was love's sacrifice I let the spotlight to shine on him. I suppressed my need for personal growth in exchange for being a wife. Both my spouse and I worked full-time jobs sharing some of the responsibilities in the home. Not completely a reciprocal relationship. My life revolved around him and his wants. I did what I had to ensuring he was satisfied. I did so without questioning any of it. In fact, I rarely objected to his decisions on anything. My love for him was greater than me.

There's no blame to pass here because it was my responsibility to make myself heard – I never did. I thought being a good woman meant agreeing with my husband's decisions. His opinions were mine and resistance had no place in the household. Disregarding to see the value in what I added to the partnership diminished my self-worth. Wearing my insecurities like a quilt further squashed my self-esteem.

Imagine years of holding back until eruptions start to shake the ground you stand on. Signs of trouble flared up when I began taking back little pieces of myself while married. Girls' night, social outings with coworkers and asking to take back some of me. When divorce showed its face, I was coming into my own as a woman. It was the nail on the coffin after a long mourning period. Lots of therapy brought a rebirth. My pride and confidence came full bloom, helped me to spread my wings. The process of getting to know the woman without a man was terrifying, at times lonely but I'd never take it back. I have committed a great number of bleeps. Let's say more than I can count, all derived from bad decision-making or naivete. Today, I am in a better place despite those badges of honor, as I nicknamed them. There's no greater beauty than owning who you are and being loved with all your flaws. Let yourself be seen in real color. Do not be afraid or intimidated by what others think. No need to hide your imperfections. The individual cracks are what makes each of us extraordinary. No two are alike. You, me – we're all in charge of our own journey. Bumps and bruises on the way up are part of the adventure. We are gifted a chance to start over just by taking that first breath in the morning upon waking up. If we can try to look at divorce as an opportunity to re-evaluate how to improve life then it might open a window to hope.

Show Gratitude by Being Kind to Yourself and Opening Your Heart

Marital separations or any breakup can cause great sorrow and anger. We can feel both emotions in no specific order or length of time. Truthfully, hopelessness took residence in my soul for several years. The dissolution of the marriage was extremely painful to deal with, not knowing how to fix me was the worst. There were days I'd wake up with heaviness in my heart. Other days, I felt ample rage capable of shoving an army of men. I was drowning in feelings of abandonment caused by the one person I thought would always fight for me. Ain't that a kick in the ass! The departure from a marriage left no room to love, leading me to build a moat around me. I had an instinctual need to protect myself from love so I would not hurt again. All the emotions in play were ideal for a destructive vortex that could swoop me into a hole of negativity. I desperately looked for something to believe in, a reason. Anything that would help make sense of all this. Time took me through a passageway of events, eventually pushing me through to the other side of the pain. I assure you that darkness gives way to light if you let it. Independent of everything happening around you and what's been done to you, if that is your situation. You make the ultimate decision to get out of your own way. Stop the wheels from turning with you under it. You start letting go once you forgive. Absolving myself meant that I had to stop the self-punishment. Poor choices and decisions add enormous weight on our shoulders. The guilt carried from failing to make things work stopped me in my tracks. It had me seeking as many distractions as possible to propel wellness.

I decided to take up a new project. Exhausted from the ups and downs, it was becoming obvious that I needed to bring back to my heart positive currents. Returning to the books seemed like a great idea since reading had been an enjoyable pastime. I read book after book. Reading on any subject that could be found to educate, uplift or bring enlightenment. Through reading, I picked up messages that stayed with me. Words are a powerful tool that can be used for good or evil. The right words put together can make a significant impact on our minds. Not wanting to forget these quotes or phrases from great reads, I began to write each down on a neon color post-it. I wanted to make sure that these messages were consistently visible to me. They say, if you hear something enough, you start believing it. The Post-Its found a home on my bathroom mirror. Months into my beta project, I walked into the bathroom only seeing eyes in front of me. The wall of notes became my temple where to pray. Increasingly stronger, it was the day I regained the feeling of gratitude. The last note to cover the mirror in its entirety read in caps, "GRATITUDE."

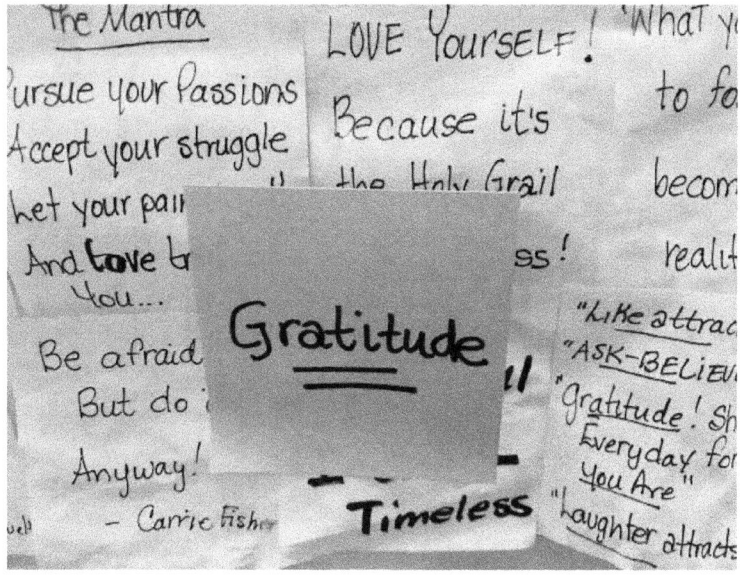

The cycle of mourning was coming full circle. Succumbing to the agony of heartbreak and beating myself up was done. Healing entered my world because I was inviting it in. I was enough. Ready to fight for survival, again. I made a conscious choice not to let anything take me out. I loved my daughter with every fiber of my being but the self-love I was experiencing pulled me over to the other side of fence - back into existence. I was thankful for a chance to start over. Watching the news every day gives us a reality check. Thousands of people around the world dying. Murders, shootings, cancer, heart attacks, accidents, all leaving families missing their loved ones. Those statistics alone should make us all feel grateful. Accept every breath as a blessing because it is a true gift not all of us will get tomorrow. You are entitled to feel sadness, worry or anger when life throws a curveball. Rise above this moment to see the intangible. That's where true happiness lies. Show gratitude to others, but mostly be good to the person standing in front of the mirror.

The labor does not stop when you have the epiphany. Waking up from a divorce nightmare meant giving up a fantasy. I had to let go of the illusion of happily ever after which, by the way, is a tale as old as time. The concept Disney planted in our heads during childhood isn't true. Love is real, it is out there, but never is it perfect nor does it come in the form of prince charming. It takes work on both sides. When fate doesn't coincide with what you wished, it can get ugly. Especially, when you throw money into it.

Money and Divorce

Divorce comes with a full set of luggage. Life keeps moving while you are rummaging through your personal bag of emotions. There is much to tackle during the ordeal – some of which we can't afford to put off for long. One of the biggest concerns is how I'd manage financially coming from a dual income household to living off one paycheck. Challenges exist whether male or female, however, in a large number of cases, men are the main breadwinners. In June 20, 1963, the United States passed The Equal Pay Act. The amendment to the Fair Labor Standards Act of 1938 was signed in an effort to end the unequal pay based on gender. Currently, women still face similar disparity in wages. Median earnings show a woman earns approximately 80.5 cents for each dollar earned by a man. Let's consider the financial impact this fact can have on a couple separating. The transition from a dual income household to single can be devastating for either side unless support is adequately addressed by a legal agreement or court. Therefore, if left unprepared, a woman can suffer major financial hardship when households are split. Alimony is recorded back to the Babylonian Code of Hammurabi created to ensure a spouse's support after divorce. It was to assist with living expenses such as food, wardrobe, and shelter. It continues to be awarded in courts today to the lower-paid spouse and is separate from child support. The child support laws vary from state to state. Unfortunately, contributions from the non-custodial parent (parent not living with the child) is relatively minimal. The amounts designated for child support don't necessarily match up to the true cost of raising a child. Usually, it's the woman left to care for the child or children in a single-income household. The financial hardship experienced by many leaves a huge mountain to climb.

The topic of money adds fuel to the marital fire. Some couples have too much of it; others not sufficient. In the middle are couples who put in equal efforts and feel strongly entitled to walk away with what they brought into the marriage. My parents legally divorced in 2005. Unofficially, they went their separate ways long before. The youngest of four children, my brother was 25 years old. We did not benefit from any alimony payments or child support. History repeated itself with me, except my daughter was 4 years old when my separation occurred. My desire to get out of the toxicity of divorce was greater than any compensation awarded. Therefore, I walked away without petitioning for financial assistance of any kind.

Everyone will have their own opinion on your situation but you have full autonomy. Your decision is the one that will count at the end of the day. I was filled with all kinds of fears about how to make things work with one income. Thoughts of how I'd cover living expenses for myself and child terrified me despite having full-time employment. Initially, I wasn't sure whether I was coming or going until one evening. Reality has a funny way of smacking you in the face hard. It will get a reaction from you if comes at you from the right angle. A couple of months into the separation, my finances weren't in order. Residual debt caught up after ex's departure. Between car payments and utility bills not to mention NYC apartment rental fees, I knew I was knee-deep in financial quicksand. I came home from picking up my daughter one evening to find an eviction notice on my door. Quickly tearing it down and getting us into the apartment I walked into my bathroom. After getting her settled, my first thought was, "God, please tell me what to do. Give me the wisdom and strength to figure out what's next, please." Tears came down incessantly, and I lost my breath for a moment. I heard a knock on the bathroom door. My daughters calling, "Mommy, I'm hungry. Can we eat now"? Reality. I wiped sadness from my face. Opened my door to see her sweet, defenseless smile – a million reasons to fight, not just for me, but for baby girl. It was one of many long nights while I came up with a short term plan. Within a week I acquired a personal loan to pay the overdue rent bringing bills up to date. The following month I got by with help from a sister, brother-in-law and a friend who moved us out of our apartment. We relocated to a safe, modestly priced rental in a nearby Connecticut town. It took me out of my comfort zone in the city but provided an affordable lifestyle. It wasn't my preference but it wasn't about me any longer. Our livelihood depended on me making sense of the numbers at all cost. I got to know a lot about myself through that experience. The situation further empowered me as a woman. We also made some great new memories.

How we deal with situations can change the outcomes. However, difficult, there are basic steps that can prove useful when potential problems arise. Begin with these initial steps to help save your financial sanity regardless of which spouse initiates the legal proceedings. It will not be simple to do this during a highly emotional time. Keep in mind - it is imperative to prepare so you can fight these battles properly and intelligently.

Unclog Your Mind

The key to getting through the hurdles is to keep a clear head. Humans are emotional beings. It's our feelings that separate us from robots. It is our passion for love, power, and freedom that helps us forge new roads as we work against the injustices that revolutionize groups of people. Take a minute to consider the emotion evoked when we believe in something. It can be the same force that might drive anyone to madness. It is extremely hard to make sound decisions if we're full of intense stress or anger. Therefore, during the turmoil, the best action to take might be none. Whether it is you or your spouse initiating a separation process, step away from the situation. Clear your head of the noise around you to find your ground. Nothing productive will come out of anger. Unfortunately, this event has the potential to spew resentment, revenge and ill-intended behavior if either party is jaded by the filing. You might ask yourself, how do you deal with a narcissist, jealous or angry ex? The first thing to do is to make sure that your life and the lives of the children (if present) are not at risk of danger. It is hands down the principal factor to making decisions relating to how you will proceed with the dissolution of the relationship. Granted, there will be situations where peril is not foreseen. In some cases, there is the possibility past irrational. If a risk is determined, seek assistance from family and authorities to plan next steps. Otherwise, catch your breath to strategize. Plant your feet firmly on the ground, assume one day at a time. It will be easier to muster up the game plan if your head is on straight. The key is to separate emotion and action which is not easy to do. Will you have days that feel like everything is just too much? Yes. Pause for a moment and continue to cope. You will see weeks or months go by showing glimpse of improvements. Healing begins to cure the hurt. Clarity produces a better outcome, particularly when a fault line starts to show its cracks. Inner calm blazes a faster trail to peace—faster than destruction ever could do. Each of you will have a different scenario to work with but keeping a cool head will help in most situations. Think then act - reacting in response to another person's emotion can have negative consequences.

Don't Bury Your Head in the Sand: Assessing a Picture of the Current Situation without Blinders

Hopefully, you now have a cool head holding an idea of how your bills will be paid. Gather all financial information and documents. If you haven't yet, educate yourself about every detail of the finances. This will make navigating the next phases more efficiently. Open your eyes to the realness of your situation. It will not serve you well to bury your head in the sand. Take a step back to look at your life ahead, there is plenty yet to live. Evaluate what is happening. Human beings have an incredible spirit along with the will to survive. Contemplate a few of the greatest survival stories. It can provide a glimpse of the inner capability we all possess to overcome adversity. We're able to withstand some of the biggest physical, as well as emotional challenges. If there is a chance you can sit with your soon-to-be ex and agree on any points then a discussion is a good start. Mediation might be helpful to both spouses as they work towards an agreement, possibly shortening litigation time. In addition, negotiations can minimize the grueling cost of attorney fees. If you know your spouse will not accept assistance from a mediator or you are vehemently on opposing sides then consider legal counseling.

The following tips could be useful if you decide to take the legal route:

1. Decide on the type of representation you want during litigation. Attorneys have different fee schedules, tactics, personalities and accessibility. Find one that fits your requirements.
2. Maintain composure, emotions derail the objectives needed to terminate the marriage in a way that meets most of your needs. Keep an open mind for compromise. Don't go into it with a list of unreasonable demands that are aimed for revenge.
3. Do your due diligence when seeking legal counseling. Referrals are best, depending on your situation. Searching for a lawyer will require you to review credentials. Narrow the list to 3 or 4 names of choices to interview. Checking with the local bar association for complaints is a good idea. Doing the legwork in advance pays off in the end. Look for anything that can pose a conflict of interest or issue that might detain proceeding. These legal situations almost always have the potential to linger causing tons of distress. Losses augment for all parties as matters drag out leaving a trail of unhappy folks.
4. Use your best judgment when making the final selection of an attorney. Your lawyer's background is crucial when making the decision but so are your instincts. Trust you can work together to do what is in your best interest.

A Journey to Becoming the Best-Self

Do it Yourself:
Poor Divorce and Possible Options

This type of divorce is worth mentioning because it isn't highlighted enough, and it is a real issue displacing families today. There are couples struggling to make ends meet who cannot afford the legal fees. In recent years, median household income has risen a minimal percent, but is still holding just under $60,000. For metropolitan cities such as New York, Los Angeles or Chicago, many people are well below a comfortable income to maintain a family. Taking this into consideration, these couples splitting the option for an attorney can be daunting. Do-it-yourself divorces can be an option in some states for simple uncontested divorces. Each state has different laws and residency requirements for filing. It can become an overwhelming project to deal with filing petitions, tracking docket numbers and filing forms. Not to mention these activities are time-consuming. You never know how busy courts and judges will be, which can leave you waiting for hours. A good number of cases are complicated by child custody battles and common properties such as a car or home which leaves couples without no other recourse other than to hire an attorney. But what do couples do when they can't afford counsel? Poor divorce is described as a lengthy marital separation where low-income couples agree to live separate lives as they would if divorced. The disunion can last from a couple to several years until the legal divorce becomes affordable. These couples aren't left with much choice and opt to resolve the dissolution in the best way they can for their means. There are resources such as pro bono lawyers, low-cost or free legal aid. Specific requirements will need to be met for various services. It is absolutely worth looking into, especially victims of domestic violence. Calling your local legal aid office or The City Bar Justice Legal Hotline for additional legal information. You will be better positioned in a settlement if you arm yourself with the proper information. This is your life we are talking about, the extra research pays off.

It's difficult to offer a piece of advice that will work for all. There are many moving parts to every divorce. Another concern is that difficult partners can create scenarios that will make everyone miserable including the attorneys on the case. Litigation can tie up spouses for an extended amount of time. In the same breath the build-up of resentment can infuriate the most patient partner.

Spinning it Your Way: Contentious Divorce

Difficult personalities drag out proceedings by refusing the acceptance of any terms. The probability of these cases being dealt with amicably is nil. In dealing with a narcissist, prepare yourself for a lengthy process. Individuals with narcissistic personality disorder can be described as chronically self-centered, lacking empathy and with an excessive need to be right. They are likely to believe that their opinion is the only one that counts. They never take criticism well. In the world of a narcissist, only their truth matters. Their delusions of grandeur can cause serious issues and affect judgment. An excessive air of self-importance can drive decision-making, delivering an intense or angry response when their ways are not met. Divorcing this type of personality will take an immense amount of patience on your part. The key strategy is to avoid engaging your ex-spouse at all costs. They will try to manipulate you, as well as the situation to their advantage, even if it means making you the villain. It is a downward spiral if you allow this person to make you feel accountable for the bad things that happen. You are not responsible for their pain. He or she will play you like a fiddle if you allow it. It is a game of strategies. The best plan of execution is not to enter into confrontations or use logical defense. Don't reply to insults or messages of any kind from your partner. If there is a question that requires a response, keep it to a minimum or one-word answers. Don't fall victim to a conversation reminiscing of the good old days or love once shared. Lastly, you are an easier target if you give in to intimidation or fear tactics. You do not owe him. Don't believe the behavior will stop if you play nice. This is not about you. It is about their desires for satisfaction and attention. One of the best weapons to use in defending yourself from a narcissist would be to stroke their ego. If there is something you desperately need, hold back from demanding anything because it will never work. In your attempt to obtain the desired outcome, use a set of words that will convince him or her that they are the ones getting attention.

Circumstances will vary, therefore, do what is convenient for your situation. Subtlety is a powerful tool to help you manage difficulty on the road of negotiations. My ex and I had our set of challenges. We did not always see eye to eye but constantly worked at the coparenting piece. Again and again, we went back and forth in disagreement which was fine because it is part of the breakup process. Luckily, there are ways to manage situations without being confrontational or belligerent. Although it does not work for every couple, this is an example of when a low-key attitude was effective.

Drop-off arrangements needed to be modified. I could not afford the weekly added cost of transportation each weekend between New York and Connecticut. Instead of asking for a favor directly, I spun it. I emphasized that our daughter was having a hard time coming home at the end of each weekend because she missed her dad very much. I mentioned it be easier for her if he brought her home to ensure she would spend every minute she can with him. He made it so that he drove her home every Sunday night. Despite the incredibly painful process, we were both aware that placing our daughter's needs first would create positive results.

Having her best interest at heart delivered the win. Surely, some may read this and imply manipulation, it is not. I used truth delicately to bring forth a better outcome, as demands by force will not work during divorce warfare. It will be survival of the fittest. Remove emotion from the equation in order to organize a proper strategy. No matter how much you might like it to be, you are now two separate entities working for the same purpose but no longer together. When the journey began, it was wonderful because you were in love. But at any point when either of you utters the word the divorce, it's a game-changer. The object of the match is not to hurt someone you once loved. There is no trophy to win. The goal is surviving the bloodshed of the proceedings with the least amount of casualties as possible.

Yvette Bodden

The State of the Children Divorce with Children at the Center of It

Children and money are the biggest topics of conversation during separation. Although, not applicable to everyone. Many couples are forced to make difficult decisions relating to children of divorce. Effects of a separation vary depending on factors such as age, personality, and situation at home. The level of complication can be so incredibly draining that some couples decide to remain together to avoid turning their child's life upside down. Although, may be seen as admirable. It's likely not the healthiest of decisions for any of the members of a family. Children are more resilient than we realize having the ability to survive divorce with our guidance.

Marriage is tough work. There is a misconception, assuming you can wrap it in a neat and pretty package. My parents put 20 years' worth of Band-Aids on their marriage. The end result was inevitable, each went their separate ways. It took close to a decade for them to remedy the situation. The effect of staying together had on our family us was irreversible. They married young without thoughts about careers. On weekends, mom and dad tried to take the four of us out to do something fun. The two did not agree on much, which created considerable tension. We would get home to have to listen to their fighting. They mostly argued about his late-night outings with buddies. It never stopped him from doing it. He rarely thought about anyone other than himself during those days. Confrontations between them would be brutal as neither would back down. We spent much of our younger years figuring out how to avoid getting caught in their crossfire. I don't want it to seem like it was all terrible. We had our share of good days, too. Unfortunately, memories of arguments stand out like a waterfall in a desert! Sadly, no matter how much good happens to you, it's the bad stuff that sticks. We need to try and be conscious of it so we can change this for ourselves. I continue to make improvements to be the person envisioned. When faced with divorce, I knew battling it out in the ring with him would get me nowhere. My strategy was similar to Gandhi's non-violent protests. I refused to resort to physical, verbal or emotional tactics, knowing it would do nothing but set us back. Turning the other cheek drained me of will and patience. There was no space for ego. Our baby girl was always watching. Eventually, we came around to a mutual understanding. Her mental health and happiness was our greatest concern. I understand this won't happen for all parents. You learn what is the best means of communicating in your situation. Methods don't have to be conventional or approved by anyone as long as you're comfortable and get results. If you enter a custody battle, things can get downright vicious. Spouses can show an ugly side during disagreements about the child's (children's) best interest. Others may be spiteful and looking for revenge. If not handled properly, it can all get toxic, trickling down to the innocent bystanders – our children. When I sat down to consider everything in play during separation, one thing stood out for me. We could not allow our daughter to witness turbulent fights between the two people she loved most. Sadly, not everyone will have control of this part, but I knew I didn't want her to see my ugly. Research and planning helped me figure out how to address the issue. Of course, I needed to speak to the ex to make sure he would work with me. We were of the opinion that despite our decision to go our separate ways, he and I should decide on matters relating to our child. Did we agree each time? Absolutely not. Heaps of arguments ended up as a tie. We agreed to disagree then drop the matter. We did concur that a judge should not be the one to dictate what was necessary for her livelihood.

One night, I grabbed my computer and listed the non-negotiable points to support my ex spending time with our daughter. The fact we were done had nothing to do with his relationship with her. He was a wonderful father, consistently taking good care of our child. Although, he was responsible and committed, I wanted to make sure he had access to her because she was the last person that should be hurt by the breakup. We were in accord on the basics, other stuff I let go. It would have been impossible to get everything I wanted, especially the numbers for support. I created an addendum to the divorce. I bulleted all the items discussed prior to filing. The arrangement would be a legal document we would be bound by when the dust settled. Our daughter is now attending high school. I'm looking at college costs. It isn't a secret that expenses for children are astronomical. How will we the divide cost? Truth is that I didn't know. I neglected to include any breakdown of college expenses. This is a lesson for you to take away from my mistake. Nowadays, there are resources online to facilitate transfer of payments and information. Some apps have little to no fees. Smartcoparent.com, for example, helps with communication of schedules, support payments and maintain records of all activities between parents. It serves to limit contact with the ex-spouse while providing a tracking system — all of which can be useful in future court appointments, if needed. There is a lot to sort out during the split. Streamlining the process will make certain dealings easier. I decided to work through it as I go. No other choice now, will figure out each challenge as it arises. If you can, I advise you to plan wisely.

Parenting styles are one of the strongest disputes encountered during divorce with children. For myself, the rewards of co-parenting outweighed its challenges. It was worthwhile for my daughter to have her father's support growing up. Is this doable for everyone? It certainly will not work for all parents. There are a large number of couples with complicated divorces that do not allow for this type of parenting to take place. I can't even remember how many times I held my tongue or cried out frustration. It takes everything out of you to hold back. Once we understood there would be disagreements, we moved on. If it required me to cave on a matter. I did, as long as it did not require sacrificing our daughter's well-being.

Rewind to 1998: do you recall Demi Moore and Bruce Willis being mocked for their co-parenting style post-divorce? Public opinion was they were nuts! Guess what, so did my family and friends when we chose to do the same a decade later. The breakup put us on opposite sides of the fence on most issues. Bonded by love for our daughter, we felt it would most benefit her to work as a united front. It was the place we landed at the end of each day. We tried to function as a family unit within reason. Him and I did not want her to feel that she had two separate families. Graduation dinners and lunches, birthdays, and any of her wins are celebrated as a family. Great effort goes into making her feel like she has a solid foundation even if her parents aren't together. Her father is remarried with two small children which she calls sisters. Our daughter has never called them half-sisters as she believes they are part of a single family unit. Holidays can be hard but we make it work. Agreeing on schedules comes a close second. I made a decision to draw my line in the sand at holidays. Initially, it was uncomfortable for me to spend a Thanksgiving or Christmas at the table with my ex and his new family. He was sharing a home with another woman. Living the dream that was supposed to be mine. However, we wanted our child to benefit from both the families. An "amicable" split meant providing her with the flexibility to celebrate at both homes. These yearly celebrations require us to respect her, not treat her like property, and instead give her the freedom to enjoy festivities equally with each of us. While our daughter was young, we alternated or split the various holidays. By doing so, it facilitated the planning for both households. There was an understanding that she would always come first. Using her as a pawn in any way was something we would not attempt during this situation. As she got older, we agreed that she should be the one to choose where or how she'd like to spend her holidays. Each of us encouraged her to spend time with the other parent. Although, not together she has grown to feel secure knowing she has the love of two parents and families that love her. We are lucky to have a self-assured, caring and thoughtful kid that has not been affected by our separation. Making the decision to leave her out of our turmoil was the best thing we did for her. Not all couples can achieve civility. If you can achieve, it will spare the kids and spouses additional distress.

As far as schedules, we discussed fair time with us. It was decided weekdays with me, weekends with him. The option of modification was always an option. Now, a teenager she maintains a similar schedule. However, she does it by choice now since she enjoys being at both domiciles. It's a good sign, indicating that she feels secure and happy with each of us. This is further proof that we did right by her, not allowing our negative emotions to affect her.

The following are three elements of co-parenting that will aid in making this a successful partnership:

1. Keep in mind, we bring children into the world, but they don't belong to us. They are not a piece of property that can be shuffled

back and forth. The child is the priority, putting them first is what will make the difference when ironing out the kinks during these arrangements. Bad-mouthing each other or treating a child as a pawn in court causes significant harm to the kids. It is paramount to remain the calm cool headed parent otherwise, it won't work.

2. Eliminate pride from the equation, it won't help anyone. It is expected the ego will inevitably take a bruising from time to time. Putting children' needs ahead of ours can mean temporarily giving up our wants, replacing them with their needs. While I was struggling with my own guilt, I had to make sure to have the best outcome. Making things at home as normal as I could under the new circumstances was essential in helping me get through it. I had to build a huge reserve of will. Dealing with everyone required loads of patience. Looking back now, the bad days outweighed the good. Trying to be the bigger person in the situation drained me. However, it taught me a lot about my strength as a woman. We have the capability to withstand the direct circumstances using these moments to empower us. Co-parenting is not for everyone. Collaborating with an ex after a breakup isn't ideal. Think of it this way: if you made the baby together shouldn't you raise it together? It would be great if it can be done under one roof, but that is not doable under some circumstances. Although easier, it's not required to have parents live in the same home to raise a well-adjusted, happy child. There are hiccups and added work to do, but it can come together with focused effort. This style will not fit all couples because endless factors can affect the outcome. It would be unfair not to caution it is far from simple. We had to keep an open mind and make compromises along the way, more than I would have liked to in adulthood. None of them regrettable because it has provided our daughter with a good foundation.

3. Getting it right will not happen overnight. The number of months or years it can take to get comfortable is dependent on a bunch of variables. Personalities, reasons for divorce, where each of you are in station of life, etc. Whatever custody arrangements and parenting styles are set. Ultimately, it should be a joint decision as long as both parents have the child's best interest at heart. *You* have the ability to determine best options without having to check with outside sources. The best attitude for both to have is understanding the child (or children) is the priority. Decisions made to benefit the children are not often wrong. We made things work for us. All done by trial and error as with everything else. There is no magic solution or a single way of doing things. You need to do what works for you, making the ultimate outcome a healthy option for all parties involved. Do not expect fairness consistently, unrealistic.

Marriages that have children have a harder time divorcing. Having children will complicate a situation as you will both need to agree on what is best for the child. The complexity of having to make decisions for your child that both parents are comfortable with should be simple. Under normal circumstances, you do what is best for them. During divorce, disputed parties may hesitate or be resistant if resentment is present. We can be blinded in the moment, forgetting the most affected - our children. They should be the primary focus. It is our responsibility to limit their suffering while under our care.

Being conscious of behaviors and reminding ourselves of everything that is important helps make the situation increasingly manageable. Kids are smart, perceptive, as well as, resilient. Concerns regarding how they will handle the loss of their normal will keep us up at nights, as it is likely the change will impact children in some way. The effects notably depend on a child's age and personality. During this time open the communications lines with your kids. If they are old enough to hold a conversation, try to pick their brain. You want to know if they have questions or concerns that need to be addressed. The better informed you are about what is going on in their head, the better it can be managed. I learned early on that kids understand an abundance. We do not give them the credit deserved. Parents should be their sounding board to guide them through the plight. For smaller children who can't speak, it's tough to figure out what they're thinking. If they are very young, there could be some separation anxiety or fussiness to deal with, although they adjust better than a middle-school-aged or teen ever could. You know your child better than anyone. They give off signals, we just need to pay attention. It will be a tall order with everything else happening during the situation. The drudgery is ongoing because you are rebuilding but well worth the efforts.

The way children are handled in a divorce is left up to the adults. However, when appropriate, it is good to ask the child about their feelings. These actions will make them feel like they matter, which is imperative. Maintaining a balance as best you can will help the family's resilience.

Dating after Divorce

You've now read about the heartbreak and hardship of separation. Sure, you have your own tales of disenchantment. Hopefully, enough time has passed that you now have a better grasp on everything. Are you ready to explore love, again? If not, it's totally ok. There is no rush on coupling up. When you are at that place, you will know. I'd love to tell you how amazing your love life will be post-cleanup of divorce aftermath, would love to share great stories about a tall, dark and handsome gentleman sweeping you off your feet and putting a big rock on it—a man who will check all the boxes on your list. Do you believe in fairy tales? I did - that's what got me trouble in the first place! Or maybe this will be the part where the plot thickens with juicy tales of sex and adventure. Well, not quite the storyline that unfolded for me. Although, there are random Cinderella stories. I didn't get the glass slipper, but I did learn to be selective in my choice-making of potential partners. The key to enduring the next round is to know what you want in a partner. Your mate isn't going to be perfect. He will unlikely possess all the qualities you're looking for in a partner. If you know what compromises you are not willing to make, it can improve the odds of getting the best possible match when ready to get back out there. Let's plant our feet back on the ground. There is one Prince Harry and he's taken! One thing for sure, if you seek love after divorce, you will find it. The greatest love affair is at your fingertips, right in front of you. You must be open to love to find it.

It's the type of love that can forever change you. Many of you have already made the discovery. My sisters called me a "late bloomer." Coming face-to-face with this type of love has empowered me, giving me a freedom unknown until now. Can you guess who it is? We'll come back full circle at the end of this women's tete-a-tete. Read on, the story gets better.

Having recently survived a 10-year relationship with a child in tow, *new love* was the farthest thing from my mind. The battle scars were still open flesh wounds that required healing. Friends expressed the best remedy in healing a broken heart by saying, "one nail drives out another nail." Although it can prove successful for some, it can complicate a number matters in other areas. A broken heart leaves you vulnerable. It's nice to have the attention but it opens you up to hurting others or yourself.

Initially, I decided to place the focus on myself, get familiar with the woman again. I realized that losing my identity was a side effect of having been part of a pair for so long. It would take time for me to get reacquainted with this person, therefore I began to date myself. Yes, it sounds utterly ridiculous but did wonders for my confidence.

Dating Yourself

The summer sun gave me renewed energy trickling a touch of hope into my day. Sunshine put a pep in my step. It helped me kick myself out of bed or snap out of a bad mood. A bright, blue sky with bursts of sunlight, a reminder of gratitude. Saturday mornings had been excruciating because my daughter spent weekends with her father. The loneliness was uncomfortable - haunting. I never liked being alone, but the sentiment is exclusive. I'm not sure if it was the feeling of not having someone's physical presence near me or the lack of emotional attention. Either way, I dreaded waking up to a quiet space without her running around the house. Slowly coming to accept she would be spending time with her father. I began planning solo activities on the weekends. My friends and family were not available every time I needed distraction. Besides, I did not want to use them as a crutch to avoid being alone. Getting to know myself was crucial to reaching my best self. It's mind-boggling how much of ourselves we are willing to lose in the name of love. Even worse, how much of our identities do we to give up to get the guy or make it all ok. Resistant to repeating history, I decided to go on a journey to find out who I was on my own.

The first solo date was the most awkward. Have you ever entered a restaurant alone and been seated while waiting for a date to join? Awkward, no? This is similar except my date was me! I didn't start with the reservation for one. Instead, I made a list of activities I wanted to try within normal parameters. It wasn't skydiving or bungee jumping. My list had movies, museums, yoga, meditation and dancing classes on it. These were all things I could potentially enjoy on my own. Although, it seems many think going to movies alone is for losers, right? Absolutely not! On my first solo date I went to see *Vicky Cristina Barcelona*. In my opinion, Woody Allen movies have to be seen zero distractions. I view his portrayal of human relationships similar to an inexplicable science experiment. It is the joining of two purely different elements of opposite properties without an idea of the phenomenon being created. In any case, great movie, the best part of the afternoon was being able to enjoy my company. There's the power behind doing things you want to do, not having to wait for someone else. The weeks following that afternoon were empowering. I checked off one activity at a time to try on my own. It was instrumental in becoming more self-assertive. I was choosing things to enrich my life in some way. Reflecting on this chapter reminds me of all that I am capable of when I set my mind to it. I decided to undo any boundaries pushing my limits safely, of course. I took on adventures, daring to do something different than before—which was anything from aerial silks suspending my body from the ceiling to shooting. A woman on a mission, I figured out what type of things I enjoyed. This led me to finding out what my capabilities were. I believe setting limits is a disservice that stunts personal growth. It had been a long road for me as it might be for you too. Life does not have one but several forks to test you. Don't be afraid to push yourself out of your comfort zone. The shedding of the old you can encourage growth like you have never seen—or thought possible.

I dated myself for at least a year before considering releasing the pheromones. Today, one of my favorite pastimes is to sit at a restaurant table for one. I study the menu while contemplating the picture of us - all the short stories we live in the span of a lifetime .

People watch as I indulge at my own pace. I don't feel we are ever completely alone if comfortable in our own skin. You can be in a crowded room and feel isolated. It's a feeling that comes from a place within. The physical aspect of being alone does not create the feeling—there is a difference between being alone and feeling lonely. I encourage you to go out there. Dare yourself to try something new. You will be surprised at the results!

I was ready to dip my beak in the dating pool despite my fears. The idea of starting over was daunting, to say the least. By the time I married and separated everything had changed in the way of how men and women interacted. Not to mention the means people were using to meet no longer required leaving the comforts of home. Dating had moved away from human interaction to the web. There was plenty of room for disasters. My resistance to use these new resources for romantic purposes seemed ludicrous, but when in Rome...

I admit, creating profiles while putting myself on the front lines for all to see made me want to gag. Knowing everything that could go wrong, I proceeded with caution. There was some strange curiosity to find out what type of traction I'd pick up from the test drive. Options were limited to Match and eHarmony. Today there are a bunch of dating apps including Bumble, Grindr, oKCupid, PlentyOfFish to name few. If you want a short rendezvous, you will find apps for that type of action, as well. Tinder is popular for many men and women. If you're looking for a distraction, it can serve its purpose. Whatever works as long as you're careful to make smart choices for yourself. You should also be reminded that everything is not always what it seems. I was toying with the idea of online dating for months. The problem came when it was time commit to a date. The moment was right for me to test the waters. I found a profile that seemed appropriate and relatively safe to make contact with, then initiated conversation.

Dating Others

Dating is a mating dance of sorts, but after being with one person for a decade, you forget how to move your hips to the rhythm. We have to learn a new game, with new players and with a whole new rule book. Who wants to do all that work? I did not. But it was the wiser choice, as I was not planning on spending the rest of my years dancing to the beat of my own drum. Humans are made for connection. We bond and communicate with each other by physical interaction. It does not always require actual contact. It can be a simple conversation with someone else. There is nothing wrong with having the desire for companionship. To the contrary, it is healthy and normal to aspire to a relationship where there is mutual attraction, physical or intellectual. Divorce does not mean you have to stop wanting these things. It is a reset to re-examine the qualities you seek in a mate. The hope is that experience and age bring wisdom. The pool of candidates should improve, though you cannot count on that to be the case. As we get older, we also become better secure of what we want in a partner, making dating extra challenging. We get pickier and set in our ways. Compromises and negotiating deal-breakers become a thing of the past. What do you do? I suggest taking one date a time. It works as a general rule in life. Meet and greets can be far and few in between or as much as you would like to schedule. The beauty of dating is you can do as much or as little to make it feel comfortable.

One Saturday night after few weeks' worth of chatting, I was ready to have a first date. We had many hours on the phone and electronic exchanges of messaging. It's amazing how texting has changed relationships. It can make some things easier. While other things become seriously complicated with technology. For one it allows people to easily fall off the map. Ghosting, (aka, disappearing acts) started becoming a trend at that point. The rules of the dating game changed drastically. An entirely new playbook was invented while I played house. A couple guys ghosted me right out of some apps. This sham caused a blow to my ego. A couple good dates gave no indication anything was wrong, leaving me with a beat up self-esteem when it hit me. Ghosting can happen to any of us. For every good catch, there are a dozen jerks. These setbacks must not stop you from living.

The perfect pair of jeans, a cute top, and black pumps completed my date night outfit. It was exciting to dress up and feel pretty. Although, I didn't want to look like I was trying too hard. I felt nervous, anxious and afraid of all the outcomes the date could have for me. All I can remember from that night is that the nerve-racking experience was nauseating. If you think about the last time you went on a date with a practical stranger, you'd feel the same. It is hard to date after being with anyone for an extended amount of time. Never imagining having to worry about any of the dating stuff again then there you are, on your way to meet a guy you were dating by phone but had not met in person, yet. I made sure to choose a place close enough for me to make a quick exit home if needed which helped ease my nerves. It was dusk, daylight set onto the windows of the restaurant-bar.

A glare of spotlights were on the table facing the window. The couple sitting down showcased their obvious love for one another. From the sidewalk, I stood still while staring at them as if it was a looking-glass of another life. My focus was on her dainty hands as she gently reached out to his face. Her well-manicured hands displayed brilliance. I am not sure what was more captivating: her happy smile or the shiny piece of jewelry on her finger. Either way, it was the worst thing to see as I walked into the pitiful first date. A connection made online in this new world of technology entered into semi-unwillingly. At that moment, I felt sorry for myself because I was once that girl in the window. I felt my ankles shackled in chains as I dragged my petite body inside. This guy had no idea what would hit him when I approached him. The lovebirds' scene made me depressed and not the best company that night. Unknowingly, he didn't have a chance in any lottery to get my full attention on the first date. I was barely able to keep up with the conversation. The night was a bust, and it wouldn't have surprised me if he didn't call again. One conversation over a single drink felt like an eternity. The mishap convinced me that I wasn't quite ready to date even though it had been a few years since my divorce. We continued our phone chats which were full of my sarcasm. His calls offered an opportunity to take the emotional baggage out of my trunk. On a random day, after a couple of weeks of longing, I called my online friend. His phone rang, no answer until it went to voicemail. There was no return call, text or email from him. Making his invisible status on the online profile disheartening. Total jerk, the least he could do was courteously tell me he was no longer interested. I was increasingly irritated during the next few days, I called every day for a week. This guy went radio silent after all the shows of attention! There was no trace of his whereabouts. In my mind, he had been super-insensitive. My gal pals partially disagreed. My friends warned talking about exes or using a guy, I just met as a sounding board and therapist was a dumb move. They confirmed I was not ready to date and advised me to try to see dating as a tool. They put a spin on it giving me a very different perspective. Their suggestion was to see it as a means to meet different people. The activity would help me explore options out there to see. If I was going to use dating to find my soulmate, it would ultimately lead to disappointment 99% of the time. The approach was logical, giving me a starting point to figure out likes and dislikes after being in the role of wife and mother for a decade. This period was about learning what I wanted for myself. Our dinners weren't just about good girl fun. They were for bonding and sharing stories, knowledge, and advice assisting us to evolve as women. Not to say the girls' night wasn't also used to decompress and unload frustrations. The camaraderie was a key element for renewing a sense of self. Friendships with smart, well-intentioned and supportive women are essential to gain further personal growth. Their guidance during this part was instrumental in avoiding some of the pitfalls of dating.

The ghosting incident left a sour taste in my mouth hindering me from getting back out there for a month or two. It was a lesson I carried with me into the relationships that followed. The experience encouraged me to bounce back into social circles. Not exclusively looking for love which took the pressure off my shoulders. I was able to take pleasure in other people's company not always assuming it would be my next great love. There should be a class for dating after divorce. The scene has changed immensely from the way we connect with people to the do's and don'ts of dating. My expertise in the area is limited as we all have vastly different experiences. Age is one factor that can put you both at an advantage and disadvantage but don't count yourself out. Plenty of fish in the sea – just get your net ready because the amount of bottom feeders surpasses the number of good catches. In the end, the autonomy to take the wheel increased my confidence to make better selections. It also sharpened my skills as a renewed driver on the winding road of dating. I have listed some suggestions that offer a bit of assistance for the exploratory stage.

Four keys you should never leave home without when you rejoin the mating game

1. Stop Taking Yourself So Seriously! Dating doesn't have to be a destination to fulfill a childhood dream of finding the perfect husband or partner. Instead, make an effort to enjoy the ride. Just think, along the way you're bound to pick up golden nuggets bursting with interesting moments to fill a lifetime of memories. There will be fun in the laughter, tears in the lessons and discoveries that may awaken your soul. The experience will be whatever shape you give it.
2. You are a prize. Let him prove himself worthy, don't be too eager to please. Know your value and understand what you bring to the table. Give a little at a time but not all of you. Keep some parts of you to yourself no matter the relationship. Remain true to the person you are at your core. Don't lose yourself — authenticity is freedom. Your love should be earned.
3. You are a whole person and complete on your own. Once you know who you are as a woman, no one can strip you of your identity. Having a clear idea of what you stand for, you will then instinctively do what is best for you. As much as we love our roles as wives and mothers, that is not all we are. You are a human being of flesh and emotion. A person with dreams, desires and individual needs like everyone else. It's impossible to be all things to all people. If we show ourselves kindness, we'll be able to forgive those blemishes we are quick to call mistakes.
4. Take care of yourself first then others. Your happy will make everyone else, happy too.

Yvette Bodden

Dating in your 30s, 40s and so on...

On average, women in the United States are living longer than men by an estimated 5 years. Researchers can't pinpoint a medical reason but have labeled this unusual occurrence "the female survival advantage." In almost all areas of the globe and throughout spans of time, it is believed that when it comes to aging, women are sturdier than men. One of the major ways to help obtain a basic understanding of how aging and longevity tie into each other is by studying the oldest generations. These are educated guesses that will require years of additional study. Meanwhile, an implication of living longer is the desire to stride for a healthier, happier and satisfying life.

The challenges of dating increase with age. In our 20s, we cannot fight off the dates long enough to come up for air. In our 30s we are wiser and, in theory, smarter! Being picky as we acquire an improved understanding of our deal breakers. Heavier baggage begins to weigh on us as we approach the second half of life. This can deter potential matches for fear of having to deal with an ex's baby drama, financial or emotional distress from previous relationships. These can serve as roadblocks getting in the way of blooming romance at times. It can get too real, too soon for those not interested in complicating their lives more than necessary. Removing yourself from these situations early might benefit you.

A romantic interest could very well possess many of the qualities on your checklist, but if he or she isn't prepared to share all aspects of your life, ask yourself if they are worthy of enjoying the best parts of you. Tread lightly as it could be a sign this partner has no intention of being there for you during difficult moments. As we get older, our priorities change, as can our checklists. The tall, dark, handsome guy we yearned for might take a back seat. A partner who is stable, dependable, honest and kind begins to appear as the superior choice. Needs change as we do, forcing you to rethink qualities that were important during the younger years. Growing into personal habits and ways over the years may also make a person stubborn. I've met older men and women set in their ways, vowing never to commit to living with anyone. The resistance to making the compromises necessary to accommodate a partner are too much to handle in the later years. There is no single manual instructing us how to live. One key to unlocking your life is to own it. Familiarize yourself with the person you are and what you want should be taken to the top of the list. When deciding if you're ready for something new, it's essential to find a person who shares your relationship goals.

All of that said, it is possible that dating later in adulthood can be easier. The pressure of starting a family or having children disappears at a certain point. Biologically, we are granted a specific period of time before our bodies begin to show wear and tear. The odds for successful reproduction decreases with age for men and women. This limits options for having children midlife. Our energy levels also become a factor affecting our decision when thinking of raising babies later in life. Among the benefits of late-life dating that make it appealing is the increased sense of security gained from experience. There is higher certainty of what we're looking for at this point, which helps to weed out the bad seeds. In the likelihood that we find ourselves in a less than desirable situation, we take on a no-nonsense attitude. This can be tricky but liberating to men and women who feel they have no desire to put up with anyone's bad behavior. Late-life dating is definitely making a comeback as people enjoy longer lives. Marketing has grown for the aging population. Senior dating sites and pharmaceutical companies increasingly target the older generation demonstrate all kinds of activities that are happening in this age group. The number of grey divorce in the United States is on the rise. Couples over 50 years of age are uprooting their lives to find new ones. As women continue to break away from traditional gender stereotypes to claim individual identity, we'll see more of them empowered by making the difficult decisions such as initiating a departure. We should not be surprised by the continuous change in the dating world as a result of the transition.

Dating and Sex

Is there sex after divorce? Of course, as much or as little as you choose! You don't die and wither away because you've signed divorce papers. Human beings have a physical need to satisfy their sexual desires. Exercising a healthy appetite for sex should not be shameful at any age, it's natural. Whether in early, mid or late adulthood your libido will knock once or twice looking for you know "what." The "who" is more of a complicated puzzle to solve. Perhaps you've been in a long-term marriage or relationship. Time together creates a nest of sorts, bonding a couple into a tightly knit fabric. Intimacy created mesh two worlds in ways that far exceed explanation. Whether performed out of love or habit, the act of lovemaking is a collection of beautiful, forceful and intense movements that deliver the most complicated of dances. Two people coming together in such an intimate act is powerful imagery. Intertwine emotions into the intricate choreography, it can form a masterpiece in its own right. The chemistry of every relationship is as different as the people experiencing it. A couple's sex life is a private affair. Divorce breaks the bonds made during marriage. Sex can be one of the most difficult challenges to get past after separation. You spend years showing one person the most vulnerable parts of you. Until one day, that part ceases to exist. The event may happen progressively or abruptly, it is often a shock to the system. The vulnerability and comfort felt is now replaced with fear and embarrassment when face-to-face with a new partner. It sounds intimidating, doesn't it? Entering into a physical relationship with someone other than your long-time mate can indeed seem intimidating, though also exciting depending on personal outlook. Distinctions can be made when the topic of sex arises. The meaning and feelings on the subject can largely rely on such factors such as gender, cultural and religious differences, as well as individual values. Traditionally, women have been made to believe it is taboo to want sex. However, females have been sexualized throughout much of history in print ads, artwork, television, and films to name a few. It seems slightly hypocritical to objectify women then condemn them for have the same desires as men. As sexual beings, we all have the urge to be satisfied. The rules of sex while dating can get fuzzy. Society has come a long way, but some old values are absolutely ingrained in the culture. We are taught that a respectable woman must maintain self-respect. Engaging in casual sexual relations is not what we teach our daughters, therefore the belief holds true for most. It's probably not the position to take while dating. The act of sex alone can provide instant gratification. Short-term pleasure can be experienced from fleeting moments of exhilaration. However, sharing the experience with someone you trust and care for will take the act to an increased level of enjoyment. There can be emotional and physical consequences that may come from having sex with a new partner. It can cloud our judgment or create havoc if not done responsibly. Adults are in charge of their own lives. A decision whether or not to have sex is yours to make. We're expected to have a clear understanding of the implications that come from it. Where is it written that things have to be a specific way? Own your sexuality while carefully exploring preferences, limits and don't be afraid to feel. Stay cautiously optimistic. You may find something new and exciting that will reinvigorate the sleeping giant, no matter the age.

Dating - Single and Lonely

Loneliness is described as an overwhelming feeling of being alone. I was trying to embrace the single status but had moments I struggled. For me, loneliness could be triggered without warning. It would manifest while watching a couple hold hands or during a romantic movie. It could be missing that one person who makes things feel better after a bad day. Or the void of not having a special someone to share good news after something great happens to you. It was not having a witness to my life. Someone to kiss me softly good night, knowing he will be there the next morning when I rise. Whether never married, divorced, children or not, we have all felt a lonely from time to time. But it is a temporary state; a passing moment. It will not feel this way perpetually. There is a stigma for women; if you are not in a relationship something is wrong with you. Is it possible you're just not ready to enter into a commitment? Or prefer to wait for the right person instead of electing to be in a with someone not suitable for you? Whatever the reason for your single status – own it. The belief unattached women are in some way damaged is not only judgmental but distorted. The expectation we should be married or have children by a certain age is unfair to the female gender. Limitations not placed on men, it is an antiquated burden still carried by women today. Unknowingly, this can give a woman a sense of unworthiness. We can get overwhelmed by the external pressures of society. Internalizing the feelings result in emotional turmoil making life wretched. You might alienate yourself to push off external pressures, therefore increasing the feeling of loneliness. The force of this tailspin can throw you into no man's land if you let it. If there's one thing I've learned from this journey is that our reaction to things that happen in our lives has a lot to do with perspective.

Growing up in the Latino culture provided me with customs and beliefs that I didn't always agree with, but knew my parents held many of them in high regard. Around the late 70s, I recall the family's criticism of an aunt moving in with her much younger boyfriend. Adding to grandmother's dismay were her two out-of-wedlock pregnancies. Mind you, my mother's sister was in her late 20s, yet everyone believed they had a right to an opinion about her life. The events get a bit twisted. Although, I remember asking my mother why does anyone have to get married. She stated that a woman can only claim her rightful place in a man's world if she is his legal wife. Anything other than that would be assumed useless and, as such, you'd never be taken seriously. I had no clue what she was talking about. But that was how she was raised, passing the beliefs on to her daughters.

Our culture and society dictate how women should act, dress, think and behave in public. There is an imaginary set of guidelines that may steer some of our major life decisions. We go into a state of panic if we aren't engaged by the age of 24, married by 26 and have a baby in the womb by 28. We feel guilt when we return to work after 12 weeks of maternity. We fear judgment from people thinking you're a bad mom because you did not stay home with your newborn sufficient time. Then we struggle with culpability for what the boss thinks of us when we take maternity to play the role of new mother. We question women who make a choice not to experience motherhood because it doesn't match up with old world views. We criticize wives who walk away from their 20-year marriage to regain a sense of self because she is no longer happy. What do we say of a divorcee who is 65 years old and jumping into the dating pool after years of taking care of her family? The list of examples to show the disproportionate views are endless and continue in society today.

In every corner of the world, you will encounter illustrations of the evolution of women. The roles we played decades ago have drastically changed despite society's persistence to contradict it by refusing to keep up with the times. Today's women have been COO of Facebook, Four-Star General for the Air Force, Chairman, and CEO of General Motors, PepsiCo and Lockheed Martin. We have a woman President and CEO inside one of the biggest boys clubs in America – Wall Street at Fidelity Investments. German Chancellor, Angela Merkel, is in the company of Theresa May, Prime Minister of the UK and Hillary Clinton who ran for US president in 2016 are among some of the most powerful women in politics. In recent years, women's contributions to the economy are increasingly gaining traction. Our purchasing power is rising as well as the ability to earn more, although we still make significantly less than men for the same jobs. We must continue to break cultural and societal rules because the model of what a woman should be is being reconstructed everywhere you go. Being divorced and newly single might have been a taboo years ago. In today's modern society, we should view it as an opportunity for a reboot with a better, happier outcome. This is the perspective we should focus on — not allowing anyone to diminish our womanhood because we don't have a man by our side. I learned to embrace, trust and love all that I am within the walls of this loneliness. Once I got comfortable with my solitude, I attracted into my circle the elements needed to feed my soul. Slowly, making progress towards a new and healthier phase of love.

Yvette Bodden

Love Upgrade - A New Relationship with Sage Rules

We're brainwashed from an early age to buy into the classic happily ever after—the possibility of finding one true love that will bring lasting happiness. Part of the Disney empire was built on these fairy tale stories. Hollywood has made endless romantic films with this theme, raking in billions of dollars over the years. The Hallmark channel ensures that their stories have a blissful ending. It's wonderful to believe something so beautiful can exist. Wedding planners coordinate lavish weddings to model this dream. Society embraces the unachievable goal to find and marry this one person in the world who is made especially for you. The end. When the story is over, we fall apart at the thought that we will never love again. First love is euphoric, like nothing you have felt before. When you have a taste of it, you do not want to let go because it feels amazing. What happens when relationships go awry? I believe it is then, when real love kicks into gear. It is the point, where reality sets to show you that love is work. It takes effort on both sides but still does not guarantee a happy ending. It does not mean life ends. It is an opportunity for a fresh start. Do overs have their advantages. Life is full of cycles. I suspect they are there to teach us the lessons. Jane meets John. They fall in love and get married. They have a baby (or not). They all live blissfully together. So, did you hear it? I did—the screeching sound of a hard, abrupt stomp on the brakes! Life is not a storybook. It's a bumpy road with dozens of detours, crashes and stop signs for the person behind the wheel. But we are resilient, bouncing back from the challenges put in front of us. We take what we've learned, pick up the pieces and start over. Your heart bounces back too. It heals, recovering from the pain and sorrow of loss. It doesn't stop beating until you're dead. Blood continues to pump through your veins, helping it thrive.

You will arrive at a place where a new situation will present itself. A worthwhile opportunity to offer your energy and emotions. Feelings of safety, comfort, and preparedness designing a path that could lead to a concrete union. It is the first time since the painful breakup. What do you do now? Give yourself permission for a redo and with a new set of rules and improved choices. Now that you are reacquainting yourself with the new you, find the value of your contributions. It is nice to please others, but not by forsaking yourself. I just provided you with *Sage advice #1*. You have a fundamental right to happiness. It starts with you. What will make you happy? Compromising is not equivalent to abandoning your needs altogether.

Love comes when you least expect it. If you set out on a mission to seek it, you may miss out on some fun parts of your journey. Building a focus on finding new love takes away attention from living in the present. When we set out to live our best life, the goodness follows.

On December 31, 2013, love found me among a room full of people celebrating another new year. Heartbreak left a hard shell around me. One guy told me he couldn't deal with the "boulder on my shoulder." Another guy referred to me as an ice queen. He said they had not yet invented a chisel large enough to chip all the ice around me. Thinking back, I can see the humor in those statements now. I didn't see the funny in his words. I was a tough nut to crack, figured I'd give up on dating for a while. It did a lot of good for me. Prior to New Year's Eve 2013, I thought love would never knock at my door, again. According to everything learned up until this time, we get one great love. Right?

My marriage to my daughter's father was an understated event. There was no celebration of a wedding with a fancy party and expensive trimmings. It was a modest celebration to fulfill a wish. A promise to each other to care, love and cherish one another for the rest of our lives. The belief that we were joining forces to grow together and be the best we could be for our family. Possibly idealistic, but many of us take a similar vow. Of course, we propose, and life makes alternate plans for us. I am thankful my path veered off in an alternate direction. Everything happens for a reason. We might not know what those reasons are until much later.

A new love was not on the agenda, which made the discovery a sweet surprise. On that last night of 2013, I met a kind, loving, respectful and good soul. This man restored my faith in love. He demonstrates patience whenever, I feel afraid. Holds my hand when I need it. He lets me go when I want to spread my wings, knowing I will return to him. We have spent over 5 years getting to know each other, a process that does not stop. The relationship has a solid foundation of trust and honesty. There are no pedestals, no promises of a castle but there is a lot of love and understanding. We embrace one another without forcing each other to change who we are. Many of us, myself included have tried to change a partner at one point or another. A voice inside my head says, "If he loves me, he will change." You might have already heard that people don't change. What we should consider is: if you love him, then why change him? It should be reciprocal, he should love you for all that you are not what you could be. *Sage advice #2* - accept your partner as they are, do not impose unreasonable changes or conditions. Make sure early on, goals and values match up so you do not get caught up later in conflict. If mutual needs do not come up to par and you stay, this will signal trouble ahead.

For example, when a man tells you that he doesn't want to get married, he means it. Coercing him into seeing your side of things or manipulating the outcome to fit your box won't make either party happy in the long run. Men tell you what they want, we decide to ignore what doesn't suit us. This piece of knowledge has kept me grounded. I won't change who I am to suit him. If there is anything essential required, I ask for it. If certain beyond doubt he cannot provide these things for me, it is my cue to re-evaluate us. This is the point where the list of deal-breakers must be taken out of the notebook. It is imperative you know what you want— most of all, what makes you happy. If you're willing to see the truth no matter the cost, you will do right by you. This has worked for me, so far, and makes me own my truths which is really hard. We work to make relationships better, there is no manual or secret strategy. Communication is key, without it the risk of crash and burn increases with time. Does our relationship have flaws? Of course, they all have challenges. Human beings aren't perfect. Expecting your partner to be that for you is unfair. Perfection is a mirage created to mask all kinds of fears. The smallest imperfections affect a diamond's clarity but doesn't shun the beauty of the gem. *Sage advice #3* - Do not set unrealistic expectations when walking into unknown territory.

The road back from divorce is lengthy and draining. Arrival at the intersection of hope and renewal is a great achievement. Going at your own pace, you eventually find peace with things. I fought several battles before redemption. The love upgrade was finding a better fit and strong love. My crowning moment, what I'd call the epitome of fulfillment has been becoming the woman I was meant to be. The despair during the first part of this journey confronted me with various emotional, psychological and physical moments that led to unimaginable personal growth. Upgrading love is about setting smart ground rules to positively influence relationships as we move away from the past.

History Repeats - Should I Remarry?

Unmarried women in a long-term, committed relationship are often asked about future plans to marry. Divorced women will often be queried on whether they will remarry. When recalling situations in a social setting, the same question is not posed to men as often. People place an unfair and unnecessary amount of pressure on women to wed. The social expectations create feelings of inadequacy, primarily if you already have insecurities. Shortly after separation, I attended a friend's gathering. It was tough walking into those types of situations. I had a plus one for 10 years, never thinking twice about who my date would be for the night. I went from fortunately coupled to single in the corner. I suspect many readers will relate to this memory. We experience the effects of uncoupling in various settings. It can make for an awkward moment at a summer or holiday party. I was a nervous wreck when asked a million questions about what or why the separation happened. The idea that others would judge me was unpleasant, to say the least. I analyzed the mistakes my ex-husband and I made during our years together. The candidness gave me clarity on lots of things giving me a sense of sanity.

In the beginning, everything is foggy, unpredictable and highly charged with emotions. Once things fall into place – and they do! — we begin to understand the choices that led to the results. There might be blind excitement matched with unrealistic expectations when we first wed. Misunderstandings can exist within the marriage if you avoid open and honest communication. A conversation should take place in advance of the bliss you believe will take place after the celebration is over. Therefore, the answer to the question, "Will history repeat itself, should you remarry"? has various responses because of our diverse set of circumstances. History should not repeat itself if you do things differently the next time. People have patterns they tend to follow. In romantic relationships, these lay out a sort of guide as to the types of we end up selecting. It can also assist in indicating how you treat your partner and react to conflict. Recognize and learn to understand which behaviors you continuously repeat. By taking on this task, you might make it easier to break the cycle if there is any toxicity to resolve before moving to a higher level of commitment. I think having open dialogue to share partners' expectations is required homework for a couple. Relationship goals should be voiced to check you're on the same page. Things can get complicated when your desires do not align. Getting remarried is a sensitive topic for those that have crashed and burned. Each of the opposing sides have an argument for the pros and cons of taking another crack at walking down the altar. Personally, I've never felt marriage is the enemy, even with all the divorces in my family. There are couples celebrating multiple decades of together. Ask any of them what the secret is to lasting all these years. Hands down, the top answers are commitment and communication. However, prior to deciding whether to to re-do, ask yourself, "Why do I want to marry this person?" The reasons for wanting to exchange "I do's" is as important as the person you will be saying those words to on the big day. Setting all the focus planning a big day of celebration leaves us thinking less about how the marriage will work. We cannot control others' behavior. What we are able to do is manage our own expectations. Get to know who you are at the core and the needs you want fulfilled. I challenge you to truly define what you want from your partner. Consider the compromises you are not willing to make for the sake of being in a relationship. Hopefully, having these pieces in place can help chances for an improved outcome of a second marriage—if that is a thought for your future.

What is Love?

Life-changing events have a tendency to make us question our entire existence! We assume our roles then get comfortable in a particular setting until there is an alteration. Death forces us to examine our mortality. We might question how we spend time on earth. Are we living to full potential? Divorce kicks us off the whimsical amusement love ride. The Initial stage of a love affair can have us travel through endless moments of bliss until the castle is bombarded with crushing reality. Love isn't a fantasy like the ones we see on television. Approximately, half of all marriages in the United States end in divorce. It's normal to ask yourself what is happening to love. Does love still exist? Do we know what true love is, can having it in abundance save a dying marriage? If it is, then why are so many couples dissolving their union?

Love is a complicated subject, as matters of the heart can be for us. I'm going to guess if you take a poll asking "What is Love?" the probability of two people giving you the same response is low. We all experience love and describe it differently. Definitions vary from person to person because each of us has a unique story to tell. Hopefully, I'm not too idealistic if I say everyone has felt love in one way or another in their lifetime. So, what is love and how do we know when we've found the real thing? Personally, I believe it is mandatory to acquire a better grasp of love to eliminate the fantasy. We must shift our understanding to veer more toward a grounded reality.

There are many types of love. The affectionate feeling can be transmitted to a partner, child, family member, friend, career or even pet. The love we give as a mother is insurmountable. The power of this mutual love is what drives us to grow our families. There is an enormous amount of love that begins even before we meet the small being we have created. Stop to think about the feeling of falling head-over-heels for someone, it can create havoc in our brain. The unexplainable fireworks go off whenever the object of our affection comes to mind or presents itself. A chemical reaction intensified by a bunch of factors, we cannot deny this type of love is intoxicating! It can make us act irrational and bring us to our knees if we let it take the helm. But what do all these different loves for various others have in common? My own experience of love can answer this question.

Earlier this year, I took a trip to Tampa, Florida, with my teenage daughter to visit a girlfriend. One night, the three of us sat down at dinner for some catch-up time. We got to talking about relationships and love. Granted, my daughter is a teenager with limited exposure to the complexities of adult love. Her father and I separated when she was about 5, hence, what happened next almost brought me to tears. I was pleasantly surprised with her take on romantic love. We went around the table looking for the answer to, "What is love to you?" My girlfriend and I have extensive mileage on love's highway which gives us a skewed view. One could say judgment cloud the ways we think about the subject. Although, not enough that we are bitter, thankfully. Though it does make me cautiously optimistic. My daughter is younger, inexperienced, and with an open heart offering– so I thought, a purer vision of love. It was my teenager's turn to answer the question her response floored me but at the same time relieved me. She took a sip of water, briefly paused and said "Love isn't a feeling, it is an action, a choice. It's being there when things get hard without allowing yourself to give up your personal power." It was difficult to follow that statement since there was nothing else I could say that could be as empowering. The moment brought me to a realization that took me back to my childhood. Love is whatever you learned of it as a child. The romantic relationships I have experienced were mostly lopsided. Investing 100% of me while accepting a poor return on investment. I had a bad habit of putting in more than received from my relationships with men. It is the equivalent of what my mother did — she gave it all to us. She relinquished everything until there was nothing left of her to give. She sacrificed it all to a philandering husband and four young children without a second thought about her own needs. Family was her priority and first love until the tank was depleted. Divorce came much later in life, cheating her out of the chance to live out the dreams. Some of the same hopes we have as young girls sitting in our bedrooms every night. Her experience led her to settle, instead of breaking away from her norm. We all have a different normal, hers was unlike mine. Likewise, my daughter's upbringing is significantly in contrast to my own. It took many decades to pick up the golden nuggets being dropped on my path to self-love. My daughter was lucky to feel the love and security of a solid foundation at home. She is clear on the fact that I loved her father very much but was unwilling to give up who I was to keep the marriage intact. She is young but already has an understanding of one of the most greatest lessons in love: The love for someone else should never overshadow the love you feel for yourself. No one is worth that sacrifice.

So, again, we continue to ask, what is love? Love means different things to different people at various intervals of life. Love in my teens was the feeling of butterflies in my stomach. During my 20s it was a fairytale living in my subconscious with a hope of manifesting itself in real time. The 30s gave rise to a different type of love that meant sacrificing. The love I was offering was such an immense surrender that it became impossible to co-exist with the woman hidden inside of me. Arriving at my 40s, my love circle starts with me. Love is embracing and accepting everything that embodies who I am. It is honest, loyal, encouraging and willing to meet halfway. I've come to understand the importance of choosing someone whose definition of love matches closely to mine. The ways we express and see love changes from person to person. Your idea of love must meet your partner's definition to complement one another. It helps both partners to get what they need from each other and the relationship.

Looking Ahead

Years have passed since our divorce was finalized. I can tell you, once the pain of the ordeal subsides, you come to terms with the facts. At that point, the memories become part of an elaborate collage of a past. If you are just initiating the process or reeling from the first steps of the grieving process, then it's tough to imagine arriving at this nirvana. I suggest avoiding looking through filtered spectacles that encourage perfection. It's best to stay away from the idea of striving for quintessential happiness. Perfection is not a realistic goal; life is chaotic but beautiful. It is a collection of moments that include sadness, joy, hardship, and fulfillment as you travel through your individual journey.

The process took a couple of years to complete. Recovery took double the time. A healthy, balanced state of mind is incredibly hard to achieve. I married under false pretenses, thinking if I satisfied all expectations of perfect wife and mother, he would never leave. I gave up the power of being myself to appease someone else and did so, voluntarily. By no means did my ex-husband coerce me into giving up my identity. While we were together, I agreed to everything he proposed without second guessing much of anything. I was under an impression we had to share the same likes, aversions and thoughts to be in sync. A thought that lacked appreciation for the strength that comes with being authentic. I was living in a misunderstanding, thinking love meant playing twins with my partner. I gave him

A Journey to Becoming the Best-Self

everything I was during our time together. When it was over, I had no idea who "Me" was anymore.

When I found myself on my own, I entered a personal rehab of sorts. Of course, physical addiction is significantly devastating and can lead to death. I chose the word for its power because recuperation for me involved mental and emotional rehabilitation. The drug was love. I had to force myself to find the woman who had been living in silence all those years. The woman who resided deep inside the walls of my body. Difficult as it was to confront truths. In time, I found my voice.

Reclaiming my identity required I reboot. I wasn't sure where to begin the process. But I knew the journey to my best self would include a set of questions and tasks to help untangle the mess I made of myself.

I began with these 4 basic but essential steps setting the blocks for my rebuilding. It worked for me, maybe it will help you.

1. Ask yourself, "What brings you genuine joy and fulfillment?" It sounds like a generic question that many of us might not have the answer to, especially after such ordeal. We spend a lot of time trying to please everyone. Being swallowed up by the daily struggles leads us to forget, what is it that genuinely creates happiness within.
2. Start a journal: You don't need to have an overflow of emotions on paper. If you would like to, do it! A good purge without witnesses can be cleansing. If not, I'd suggest you jot down one goal. It can be big or small, as long as it works toward unraveling your potential. The goal should be to get you closer to your true self. Give it a deadline of a week, a month – up to you. For me, the first goal was doing one good deed. By doing so, I was able to shift the focus off

me and reconfirm to myself (not anyone else) that my heart was kind. It's not that I forgot. I had hidden my true self for so long, I wasn't sure my empathy button still worked. Divorce affects you in countless ways. Closing yourself off from emotions can leave you branded. Luckily, the burn is not a permanent mark.

3. Create a grateful jar: Each day, I picked up my daughter from school. I asked, "How was your day?" It's the age-old question that we often are not sure how to answer. I decided to change the question to: "What was your best and worst today?" We all have them each day. I wanted her to see that for each small thing that might go wrong there is a good thing to counteract it. I think it is part of the balance of things. There is a great deal of benefit in gearing your attention towards the positive. It promotes overall wellness creating a general mood of rightness. Today we keep a jar at home to remind us of all those things we have to appreciate in our lives. We write them down to remember to say thank you then stick them in the jar. Every December 30th we sit down after dinner to review all the moments to be grateful for in life. We must remember that waking up breathing each day is a moment of thankfulness not to be taken for granted.

4. Make connections: For a long time after breakup I internalized the feelings about myself, my ex and our choices. I felt like a failure, a sham for not giving myself the respect to fight for me. Admittedly, the shame of divorce weighed on me. It was difficult to talk about what I was experiencing — until I met a cab driver on my trip home from a work event. I got in his car and must have been looking pretty miserable because he asked with concern, "Miss, are you ok? Your eyes hold much sadness in them." Of course, I abruptly said, "I'm fine, thank you." And quietly went back to texting. He proceeded to tell a story, unwarranted, of how he had just returned from seeing his 14-year-old daughter in the hospital. She was in

stable condition, but being held for psychiatric observation after an attempted suicide — the result of a bullying situation at her middle school. I removed my phone out of lap and listened to his sorrow. I'm a parent of a child close to his in age. I am blessed to go home to my daughter each night to find her in good spirits. I had just met this man, never seen him. Likely never to encounter him, again. But that evening, I connected with a father, a parent who wanted the best for his child. It had been a while since I experienced that form of human connection. We all need connection to evolve as human beings. Living without it can lead to emotional isolation affecting your overall health. If you find yourself withdrawing, push yourself to reconnect with one person. For me, listening to a taxi driver tell his story made me feel empathy, gradually making me want more of that feeling. Engage in the world, everyone's starting point will be different. Place one foot in front of the other – one connection at a time. It will teach you about how much love your heart can hold.

Discover Your Passion and Find Purpose

Most of us wake up to the same routine each day. We get up around the same time except for the occasional taps to the snooze button. Some of us work at home while others commute. We do it every day with the expectation that we'll return home and do it all again the next day. Do you smell a groundhog? Yes, we pretty much live the same day over and over again. It is everyday living for most. Can you imagine doing this, but loving what you do or where you go each day? I'm going to guess the majority will think it's a pipe dream. Sadly, it might be for a lot of us because we have bills, mortgages or rent to pay, kids to take care of, responsibilities to uphold. We also have to make sure to put food on the table each night! Realistically, we are just thankful to have somewhere to go each day so we can take care of ourselves and our families.

I've dealt with the loss of loved ones throughout the last decade, as we all have at some point. When someone is taken away, it tends to feel they are gone too soon. It is natural to take inventory of your life. I believe that we all have done something similar. Death makes us face our own mortality. You may wonder, why bring up the topic of loss? We live day to day and function as best we can. We stay on autopilot a chunk of the time leaving us floating through life until it hits us – is this all there is to life?

My *Aha!* moment came around the end of May 2017. I was

surrounded by supportive family and friends, as well as strong health and buckets of love. I'm thankful that with the help of decent employment, I've been able to provide well for my daughter. Everything seemed pretty stable, keeping me content. The issue - I didn't feel like my heart was full. I felt uninspired with an unexplainable void — an uneasiness that kept nudging me over and over. I was unable to put my finger on the reason why and the uncertainty left me with discomfort. The answer came organically in an unraveling of events leading to my purpose.

One afternoon, I received a call from an old friend who was working on a business venture. He mentioned he had developed an application that would help single parents looking for help sorting financial matters while co-parenting. Himself a divorced father of two, I thought, who better to know what is needed to make this a success? I kept in touch, excited to learn additional details for rollout of his idea. During one of our conversations, he suggested that I write a blog for his site. He was looking for an article from a divorced parent's point of view. The most appealing aspect of it was that I could write it from my point of view. The piece was personal, honest and came from a real place. I submitted the blog a couple days after his request. The writing gig turned out to give me one of the most satisfying feelings I had ever felt. The better news was that within a couple of days, the blog posted hit 2000 views! People wanted to read about the smart steps to getting finances in order post-divorce. The accomplishment of helping someone in any way is fulfilling. Writing about my romantic, personal and private experiences to help others in their journey is awe-inspiring. It's amazing how the power of words can move and comfort people. We feel it when reading our favorite authors. Experience it when listening to uplifting speeches or songs. Moved when we hear a quote that lingers well after it's been put out to the universe. Words can inspire change in people. I realized the power of stringing words together. It could be used to help empower others, hopefully making a difference in other people's lives.

The inner circles of my business and personal affairs have put me in contact with many people. Most of them seem satisfied with their lives and careers. Others drag themselves to jobs each day, unwillingly. Living a life of monotonous responsibility wins most days. A handful of people, however, genuinely love what they do. These individuals are passionate about learning everything they can in their field to lead intelligently. They want to make life better, want to do better. It's more about what they can do for others than what others can do for them. It is an ideal not all aspire to or comprehend. We enter adulthood with a sense of duty to family, forgetting and consequently giving up our dreams. We get lost in the shuffle of reality. Eventually, the reflection in the mirror begs questions: "Why am I here? What role do I fill in the improvement of society?" A purpose is bigger than us. It demands that as human beings we figure out how to contribute to the transformation of one person or group's life. You may find during this exercise of exploration a discovery causing strong excitement; an unknown skill or talent to help catapult you to the next phase of your journey.

There is a world of possibilities to see and experience. Inevitably, we are going to get a taste of the sweet and sour. Opportunities will present themselves, the ability to see them is there if we keep our eyes and heart open. Nothing is permanent, including our existence. Shouldn't we make the most out of the time granted on earth? Shouldn't we use the energy to light up life and the world around us?

Coming back from divorce isn't easy. There are numerous setbacks along the road to recovering emotionally. The decision to stop being a victim of the pain is necessary to heal. Time frame will be upgraded or modified where necessary. We have no idea what our expiration date will be nor do we have any guarantees of the type of life we'll have, even when we work hard for the things we want. Outside of being introduced to my best self, I'm making each day count. The awakening experienced after divorce has provided me with endless gifts. I'm using these to pay it forward by presenting others hope, encouragement and empowerment to seek truth in their lives.

Epilogue

Your life is a full-length novel made up of many episodes with endless drama. The intricate twists and turns are played out by thousands of characters. The people we encounter throughout it, play a role in our story. Simultaneously, these same characters are developing their own tale. It's a gift when you consider the trajectory that unfolds from birth. We're born into the world innocent of any wrongdoing or prejudice. As we grow into the life created for us, things progressively change. We receive our values and belief system from what we learn at home. Culture plays a significant role in how we view the world, making a lasting impression that follows us throughout our lives. Until we begin to experience life independently. The interaction with people and the world outside takes effect. This is when our actions and decisions as to how we behave and live are influenced.

While writing this book, I picked up a lots of information from reading several books. There were books on self-help, leadership, memoirs and re-reading classics like "Breakfast at Tiffany's" and "To Kill a Mockingbird." The collection of literature had a profound effect not just on my writing but also in the way I think about life. The knowledge absorbed was useful as I tried to make sense of it all. It's like a game of connect-the-dots or finding the best shades to finish a painting. I have been trying to create a picture for the readers of this book. The thoughts began to pull together giving me a clearer purpose. My existence in its purest form now means something larger than the physical state I'm living.

A pyramid is described as a grandiose structure with a base, slanted sides that unite at the top, built from stone. If I break down my life into three parts – past, present, and future — it forms my own pyramid. We all have our own monument. My childhood and early adulthood mistakes led to some dubious choices. I consider myself lucky that none of my faux pas were irreparable. I had my adulthood to catch up, though. Later in life, the heartbreak of divorce caused my depression, consequently taking me through a vortex of agony and despair. Emotional turmoil was in the company of external influences that forced me into a downward spiral. Relocation after separation along with a temporary loss of employment due to layoffs after 6 years at a firm, was, to say the least, devastating. It took me away from everything that was familiar. These were challenging times but now I look back on every hurdle I jumped over, appreciating my strength and worth as a woman. All the events leading up to this minute serve a purpose. These experiences have provided a foundation. They have helped shape who I am today — but none of it defines me. My past has served as preparation for how I embrace my present.

I can enjoy the current state of my life because of the moments I've had to endure. I try to live with gratitude. We tend to get so preoccupied with planning our future that we forget to stay present in this instant. Once you arrive at a page in your book where you embrace the difficult times that have transpired in life, you gain clarity. It's essential to accept the pain and let it change you. If you set it free instead of holding it hostage you can begin healing. Consequently, guiding you out of the negativity. This all sounds impossible, but it is not. That said, I will not deceive you into thinking it is a piece of cake. Likely, it will be one of the hardest things you will ever do, potentially draining you. Not to mention it will take time.

How long? We do not know for certain. The blocks you're building now will make for a brighter future because you will be stronger. Hopefully, renewed strength will fuel your energy to work towards the future envisioned.

Time Waits for No On

Have you ever asked yourself, Where does the time go? Ready or not, life keeps moving. It does not ask for your permission to keep running. There is a relentless pursuit to get where it needs to go. The best way to deal with what feels like time traveling at the speed of light is to keep moving with it. Our lives don't come with a stopwatch, giving us a chance to press pause. Once you start the race, there is no stopping it. We get some rest stops along the trail to help catch our breath. I think the pause is actually, time granted to figure out the pieces of the puzzle bringing us closer to our purpose. Years ago, I lost a loved one to cancer. There have been subsequently several more taken by the same killer. Most everyone has lost someone to this terrible monster. It's cruel in the way it uses slow death to take away a being's spirit. If you look up the word death in the dictionary, it will give you three different definitions. Ultimately, life is limited for all. When we are young, we believe we have nothing but time. The euphoria we experience during our youth can make us feel superhuman. Reality is, we're mere mortals and tomorrow is not promised. Death is a painful reminder that life should not be taken for granted.

    The first time I knew of death was at the age of 14. He was the most popular boy in school. Gino was a well-liked school athlete, good looks and tons of friends. He surrounded himself with all types of people. It felt like he would live forever because his energy was so infectious. Once a week after school, a bunch of us would gather at a friend's neighborhood for pizza. This particular day changed us and the way we thought of life. Gino never showed up to our gathering that day. Instead, we received word he was gone. A self-inflicted gunshot wound to the head during a game of Russian roulette. The weeks and months following that day were a shocking reminder we are not eternal. It was a reminder of my own mortality. Granted, my friend made a choice, but it didn't make acceptance any easier. Death is the end to the physical existence leaving all men on base. No more chances for a home run. We have to remain present in every moment, taking advantage and make time count. There has to be a reason we are here passed fulfilling a personal agenda. If we collectively do our part to contribute to the good of society, it will help others, as well as ourselves.

Setting out to live my best life means doing the most I can. Honestly, I don't think I began contemplating a purpose until the writing began. Many questions led up to that moment, eventually bringing me here. I had an average kid's experience in New York City. Inner-city living balanced with strict rules of a Dominican household both kept me in line and out of harm's way. Outside of the occasional teen mischief, my parents were able to run a tight ship. They did the best to provide a good childhood for us. My mother was 21-years-old when she gave birth to me. Two sisters and a brother came several years later.

I'm grateful to her every day for taking the role of disciplinarian. Having the responsibility of a child at such a young age forced her to let go of her dreams to care for our family at home while dad worked. She took any chance she got to remind us that she did not want the same fate for us. She is passionate and pushes hard but always encouraging us to shoot for the stars. A fiery Latina who is self-assured, outgoing and stands for her convictions. She helped me believe I'm capable of great things – anything I set my mind to do, I can do. I'm learning to embrace and appreciate the woman I am. Constructively, using the time left to learn as much as I can about myself and the world. Upkeep is an ongoing challenge because we're creatures of habit. Sometimes, it's preferable to maintain the same pattern because changing means effort. Time has become a luxury that I treasure as I get older, shameful to squander it. Today, I make it priority to find ways to improve myself by continuing the personal work.

Yvette Bodden

The Power in Having No Fear and Courage to Live the Life You Envision

My parents could be labeled as over-protective. Although I didn't understand this at the time, as a parent of a teenager today, it's the obvious right choice! NOT. I'm unsure of when it all began, but I became fearful of so much throughout life, hindering me from reaching full potential early on. Women are excluded from boardrooms, C-Suite positions, highest paying jobs, and men's clubs. If we raise our girls in fear, they will never believe that they can break the glass ceilings planted all over the world. We don't raise our boys that way. I'd dare to say it's probably the total opposite. Boys are raised to be fearless and tough. Do we remember hearing, "Boys don't cry"? My father preached it to my little brother whenever he demonstrated emotion or weakness. I think it was reinforcement to make sure he wouldn't fall short in the manly department. As the mother of a young adult in our society, I've chosen to alter some of what I was taught growing up. We must show our daughters to have courage with caution. They should be able to jump into an adventure using measurable calculated risk. None of us know with absolute certainty what we are capable of until our will is tested. On the path to finding authenticity, we have to be willing to live out our personal truths. We, ourselves, and our children, especially females have to brave enough to forge ahead fearlessly in search of the life we foresee without restrictions. Naysayers will be lurking in the corners waiting for your other shoe to drop. Dream-crushers will close many doors, but you can find a window to peek inside at the endless possibilities. Have faith in your power to make a good life, GREAT!

Yvette Bodden

Don't Wish Your Life Away

Remember the nursery poem, "Star Light, Star Bright?" Can you count the times you've said, "I wish—"? Many wishes are floating out in the universe. If I had a penny for every one, I might have collected sufficient for a house on the hills. Throughout the past year, I've become exhausted, now refusing to use those words. They seem to discourage me from the things I yearn to do, making me regress into a sort of limbo state. When I began writing in 2017, I had set out to do two things. The first, to help inspire, encourage and give hope to as many women as possible. The collection of experiences we gather during the course of our lives leaves many scars. I wanted to share mine for something good - to empower others. The second goal was to get published. Getting a publication anywhere is a good start when you have not been accepted. The significance in being published would mean increasing the number of people I'd be reaching with my message. My lack of understanding for the literary world would not hinder me. I accelerated efforts to get a reasonable idea of what I was getting into. It required research to navigate new territory. The work demanded me to make time. Reading became as essential as the writing. There were days I fell into "The Dip." The space we've all visited when unsure if we're going to make it. We are terrified, and anxious, and overwhelmed by doubt as to how our plan for success will pan out. Will all the work we've put in pay off? Are results going to meet expectations? Admittedly, there were fleeting moments that left me deflated. I gathered from conversations with fellow writers and reading articles that getting published was an uphill battle. Every one of the writers explained that developing a thick skin was absolutely necessary to get through the possible years of rejection. There were days that were painful, but I've learned to acknowledge and accept that there will be those people that turn down my writing. Moments like these to test my will and determination. I believe it's the universe's way of checking to see how committed I am to my purpose. The decision not to allow obstacles to discourage me is relentless. The thrust forward was obnoxious as I sent my work to dozens of contests, literary magazines, and editors that would accept a submission. The writing came in the form of short stories, blogs, essays, and articles. My goal has been to stay relentless in the pursuit of getting the words out to women. Before the end of 2017, I sat down to write goals. I listed them from smallest to biggest ideas that I'd bring to fruition before the end of the following year. It was close to the halfway point when my dip began. The next project to implement was the "Awakened-Woman" blog. Refusing to surrender my goals, I moved up the timeframe, adding pressure to deliver. However, I was confident in the work I could produce. If my writing came from an authentic and real place, then all I had to do was put the story on paper. Once that was done, I'd send it off to be read by anyone who wished to do so. It wasn't easy to undress my life in front of others. Can you imagine the vulnerability faced when someone puts their personal story on WiFi? Although, I get to choose what I write about, being true to myself means discussing the difficult topics as well. The "Awakened-Woman" blog went live on May 25, 2018.

Writing "Don't Wish Your Life Away" on a piece of paper and sticking it to the wall changed my perspective. I looked at the message on the Post-It note every day. Writing during my free time, when the world is sleeping, sometimes even when I'm sleeping! I write all the time, every chance I get because it is my passion. My purpose made itself visible. I'm less afraid or affected by rejection. It makes me work harder, fueling my determination to be heard. In late May, I wrote 3 articles. Each of these carried a very personal message. I titled them "Alive", "Time Waits for No One" and "The 3 Ways to Conquer 'The Dip.'" They all hit close to home. I left a piece of my heart in these stories. My voice transferred on to paper but these three were likely my favorite pieces. I wanted the articles to be read regardless, of whether people agreed with them or not.

The feeling was strong; I needed to make something happen. I closed my mind to any self-doubt when I sent the three pieces to Thrive Global. The online startup with Arianna Huffington at the helm was a big bite for me to chew. She was the co-founder and editor-in-chief of The Huffington Post until she sold it in 2016. I'd been reading Thrive Global since it started in November 2016. I enjoyed their positive pieces related to wellness and balancing life and work. It might have been a long shot, but I hit send on the three submissions. The site usually gets back within a week. The deadline passed on the response time but I felt the pieces had a real shot. The work doesn't stop. The writing and submitting process is endless, therefore I continued to write other pieces.

Congratulatory emails arrived in my inbox on June 28th and June 29th. The goal was to get one publication for the year. The joy of reading that three articles were accepted for publication at Thrive Global was too much for words. Pride and exhilaration came with those acceptances. I knew my work was good but now someone else did too. Since then, a total of 10 articles have been published by the magazine. On the same day, my blog turned 30 days young. I reached 1000 views from all over the world. Of course, to a seasoned blogger this number is jelly beans, but to me, it meant that I had fulfilled the list of short goals set for myself in 6 months. I projected completion to be one year. This number signified 1000 readers had taken the time to read my messages. Present day, the number of visitors has blown away my expectations. Readers have reached the tens of thousands leaving me filled with gratitude. If I'm able to lift one spirit by offering inspiration to do something different. If I can improve one life, it is progress.

I'm happy with this round of accomplishments. I'm now moving on to my last item on the list. The completion of this book for you. On so many days, I wished to write it. There were days, I could not see the light at the end of this tunnel. The present feels bittersweet because the part of me I have shared with you concludes here, doors are closing. This chapter of my life, I have held onto dearly is now cautioned to the wind. I can release it and go on to the next portion of the journey. One of the best lessons for me has been realizing that as long as there is life, there is growth. We must continue to evolve into our best self. Growing pains will appear at every corner but it shouldn't discourage us from giving everything to achieve our dreams.

Women give so much of themselves. We give our hearts, bodies, energy, even identities to fulfill a promise. As nurturers and caretakers in a society that tries to fortify families, we give it all hoping to feel validated. Our vow to love and care for the ones we value has meant sacrifices that are sometimes overlooked. Like many of you reading these pages, I've also given up part of myself at some point. The desire to be validated had been so intense that I was willing to do anything to get it. Relinquishing my power for the love of a man was not going to give me the acceptance I was seeking. True love begins with yourself. Coming to the realization that choices have consequences was painful. It put me face-to-face with one of my most powerful truths: I am the one person in control of my destiny. The roads I take will alter life's path positively or negatively. There are no regrets as every experience has provided me with an opportunity to learn. Although, in years passed pitfalls looked like failures, today they are no longer seen as anything other than life teaching me. This precious piece of wisdom has freed me from the guilt of making so many mistakes.

The idea of wishing life away is one I no longer sustain. We get a single shot with no do-overs to come back and hit restart. The decision to take the bull by the horns is something you must do daily. You don't make the decision to mercilessly forge ahead with a goal expecting to stay on autopilot. Speed bumps slow you down. You must take the wheel to drive your own success. Be prepared for those detours but keep moving towards the ultimate prize. The measure of your success is at your discretion. It should not be sized by society's ruler. Once you get to your glorious moment, there is upkeep. Don't shy away from the work because it assures continuation of life running at maximum performance. It will lead you to thrive resulting in your greatest self.

The human spirit is unrelenting when it taps into the innate need to thrive. This power is one of the many wonderful gifts we have outside our capacity to love. People have survived great tragedies due to their will. If the magic can be turned inward, imagine all the amazing things we can accomplish together. Everyone has the ability to overcome, endure and master hardship. It is a worthwhile effort. Trust that you can do it all and you will!

"Turn, I Wish Into I Will."

Appendix

If your circle of support is limited there are resources to help guide you through some of the challenges you will encounter on during your personal journey to best self. These books, articles and resources helped me open my mind and heart to the possibilities.

Extraordinary, Jessica Herrin, Crown Business, Crown Publishing, 2016

The Power Playbook, Lala Anthony, Penguin Random House, 2015

You are a Badass, Jen Sincero, Running Pressbook Publishers, 2013

The Gifts of Imperfection, Brenee Brown, Hazelden Publishing, 2010

Married to Me, Dayanara Torres, New American Literary, division of Penguin Group, 2008

From the Heart, Robin Roberts, MJF Books, Fine Communications, 2007

Eat, Pray, Love, Elizabeth Gilbert, Penguin, 2006

You Can Heal Your Life, Louise Hay, Hay House Inc., 1999

The Alchemist, Paulo Coehlo, HarperTorch, 1988

Breakfast at Tiffany's, Truman Capote, Penguin Random House, 1958

All About Narcissistic Personality Disorder, Medical News Today, Christian Nordqvist, January 2, 2018

Children Don't Get Divorced, Psychology, March 1, 2018

Income and Poverty in the United States 2016, Report Number: P60-259, Jessica L. Semega,

Kay R. Fontenot, and Melissa A. Kollar, September 12, 2017

7 Steps to Choosing the Right Divorce Lawyer, Laura Miolla for YourTango.com, Feb 2, 2014

Divorcecare.org is a ministry initiative that can assist with support. The church pastor, minister or clergy can be a resource for individuals that rely on spiritual guidance.

SAMHSA, *Substance Abuse and Mental Health Services Administration*, 1-800-662-HELP (4357)

Suicide Prevention Hotline SPH 1-800-273-8255. Counselors are available 24/7 to assist.

Local Legal Aid Society or *The City Bar Justice Legal Hotline* for legal information relating to legal resources such as lawyers, child or spousal information in your state.

Online Dating Sites: Match, PlentyOfFish, eHarmony, Zoosk, oKCupid, CoffeeMeetsBagel are just a few of the most popular sites.

Online Communication Tools for Co-Parents: SmartCoparent can help you get started for free, there are others out there you can research.

Note from the Author

Word-of-mouth is crucial for any author to succeed. If you enjoyed the book, please leave a review online—anywhere you are able. Even if it's just a sentence or two. It would make all the difference and would be very much appreciated.

    Thanks!
    Bodden

About the Author

Yvette Bodden is a Freelance Writer. She founded *Awakened-Woman* as sole blogger. She writes articles, essays, short stories and is currently working on new writing projects. You can find her most recent contributions on *Thrive Global, SmartCoparent* and *DivorceHub.*

Thank you so much for reading one of our

Motivational & Inspirational books.

If you enjoyed our book, please check out our recommended title for your next great read!

This Side Up by Amy Mangan

"This Side Up will leave you feeling relieved, not alone, hopeful, and grateful for a friend and writer like Amy Mangan who inspires us to reframe our let downs, have some laughs, and embrace life with all of its beautiful unexpected messes." –Stacy Strazis, former producer The Oprah Winfrey Show and CNN

View other Black Rose Writing titles at www.blackrosewriting.com/books and use promo code **PRINT** to receive a **20% discount** when purchasing.

www.ingramcontent.com/pod-product-compliance
Lightning Source LLC
Chambersburg PA
CBHW052048070526
44584CB00017B/2108